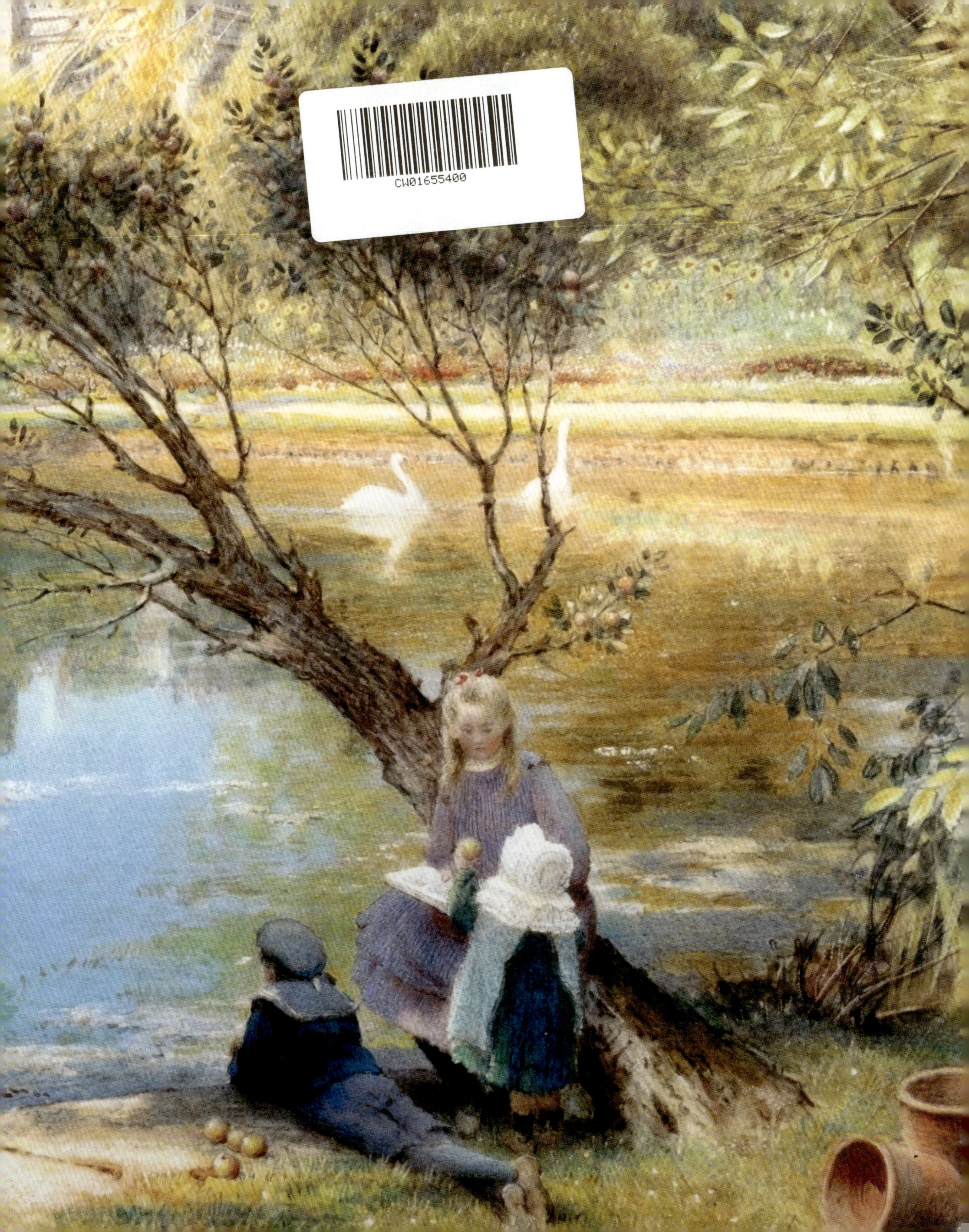

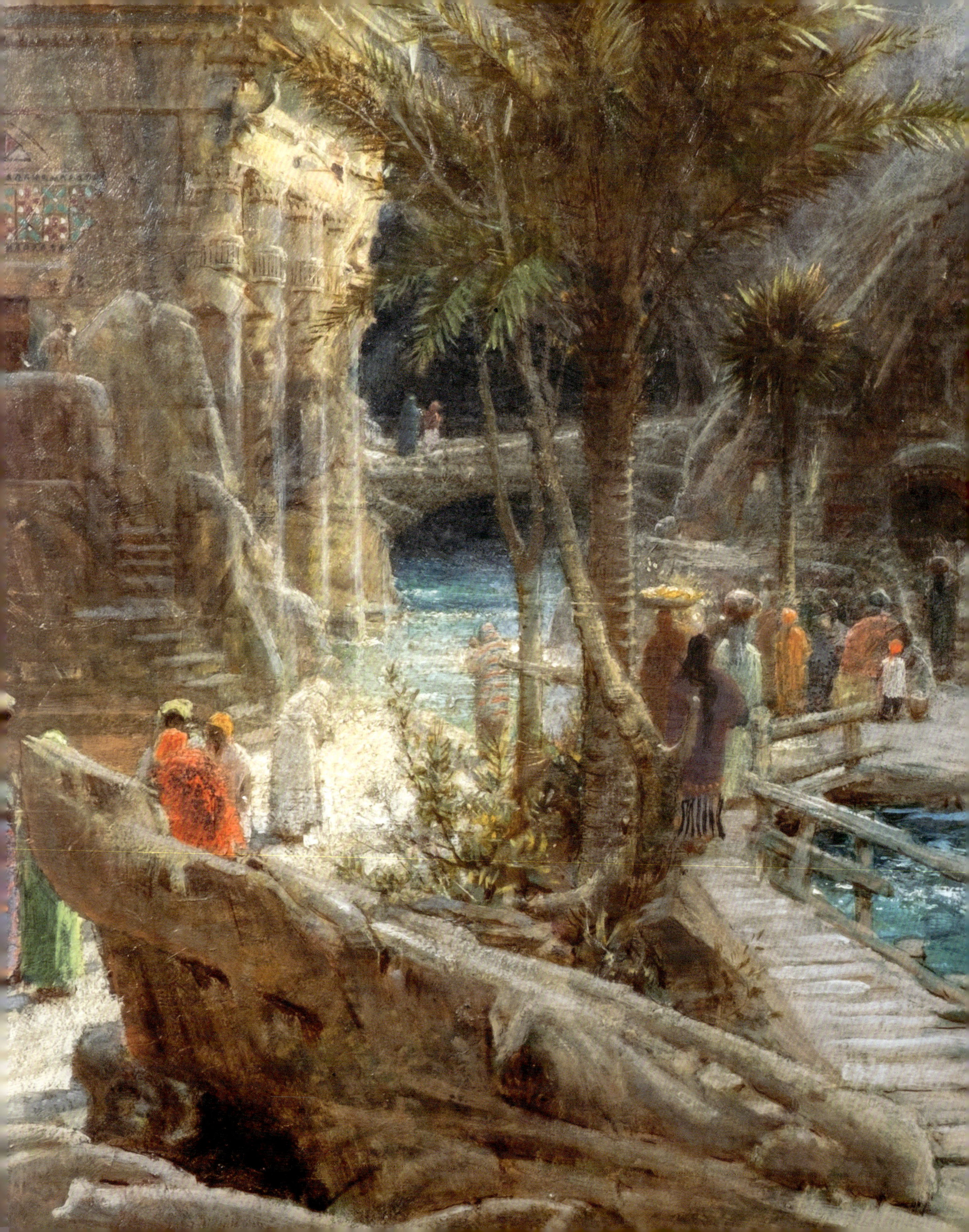

ALBERT GOODWIN
RWS (1845-1932)

The John & Mary Goodyear Collection

CHRIS BEETLES GALLERY

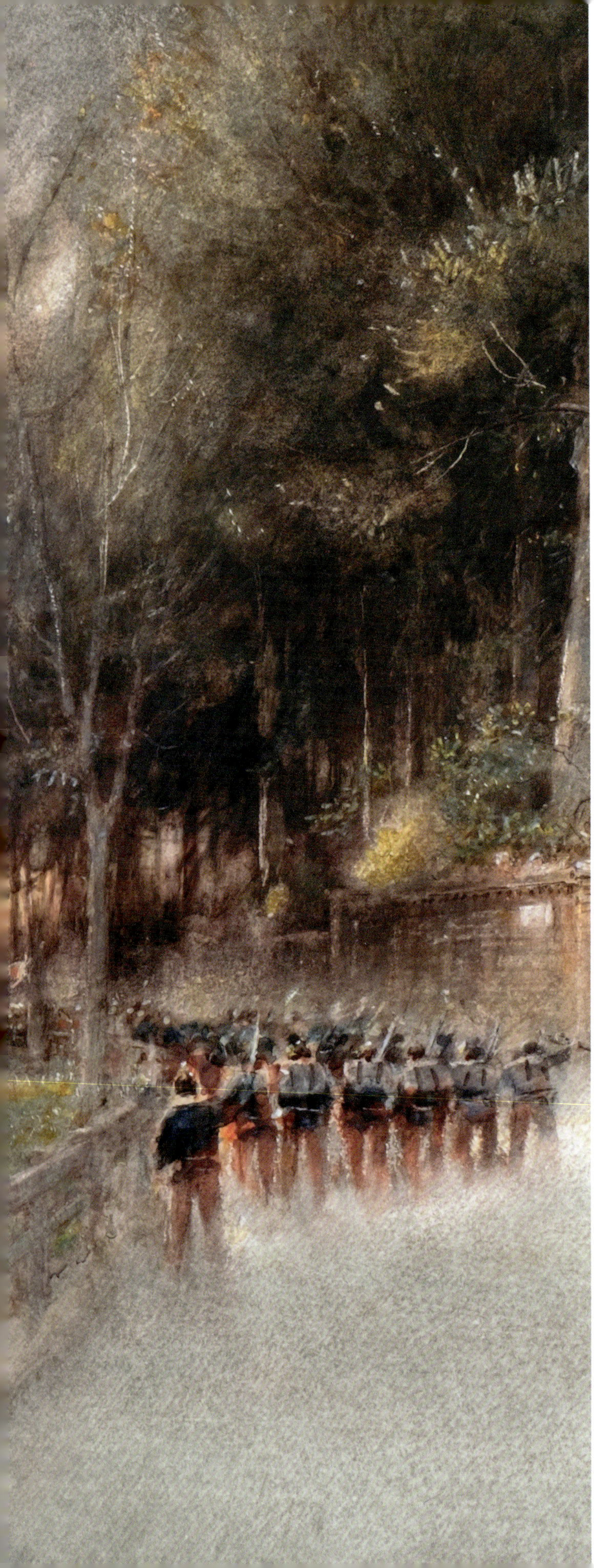

8 & 10 Ryder Street
St James's
London SW1Y 6QB
020 7839 7551
gallery@chrisbeetles.com
www.chrisbeetles.com

ISBN 978-1-914906-03-9

Cataloguing in publication data is available
from the British Library

Written by Dr Chris Beetles with additional notes
by Fiona Nickerson

Edited by Fiona Nickerson and Pascale Oakley

Design by Pascale Oakley

Photography by Alper Goldenberg
Reproduction by www.cast2create.com
Colour separation and printing by
Geoff Neal Litho Limited

Cover:
Under the Roof of the World [20]

Front endpaper:
Wells [14]

Frontispiece:
The Source of the Sacred River [detail, 23]

This page:
The Road to "Glory" [detail, 2]

Contents:
Westminster from Lambeth Bridge [detail, 43]

Page 6:
John Goodyear

Page 9:
Mary Goodyear

Pages 20-21:
Appledore, N Devon [49]

Back endpaper:
Benares by Moonlight [47]

Back cover:
Lucerne [42]

CONTENTS

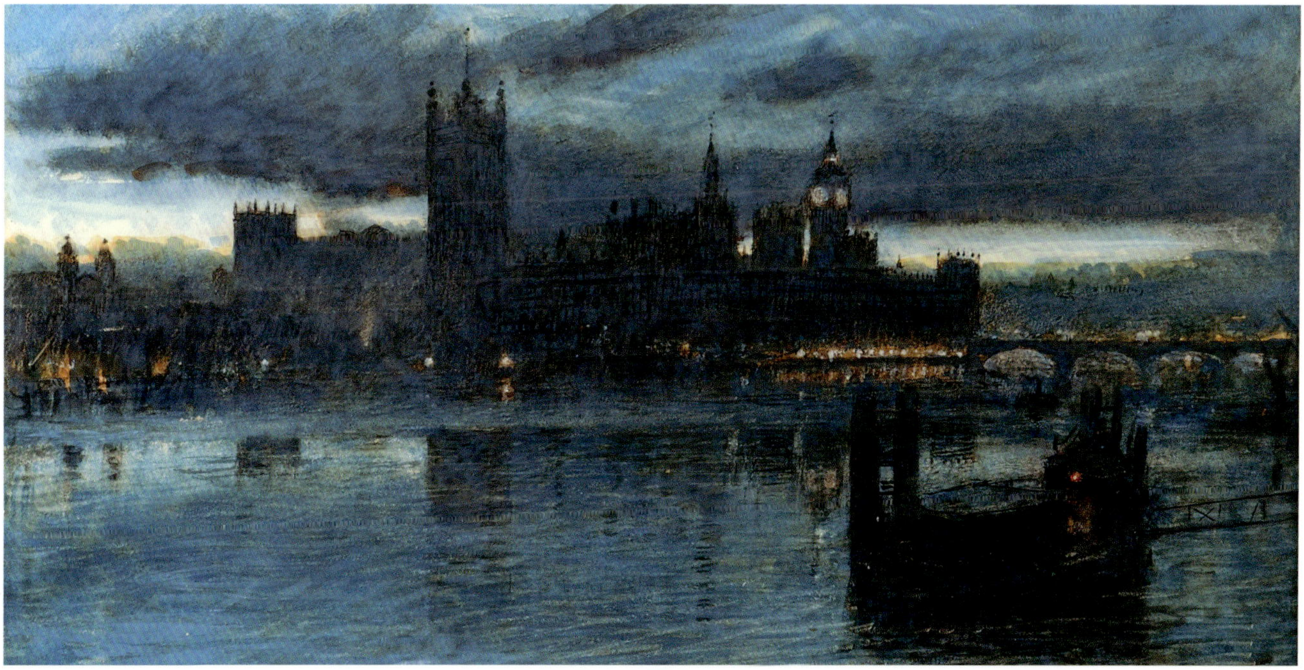

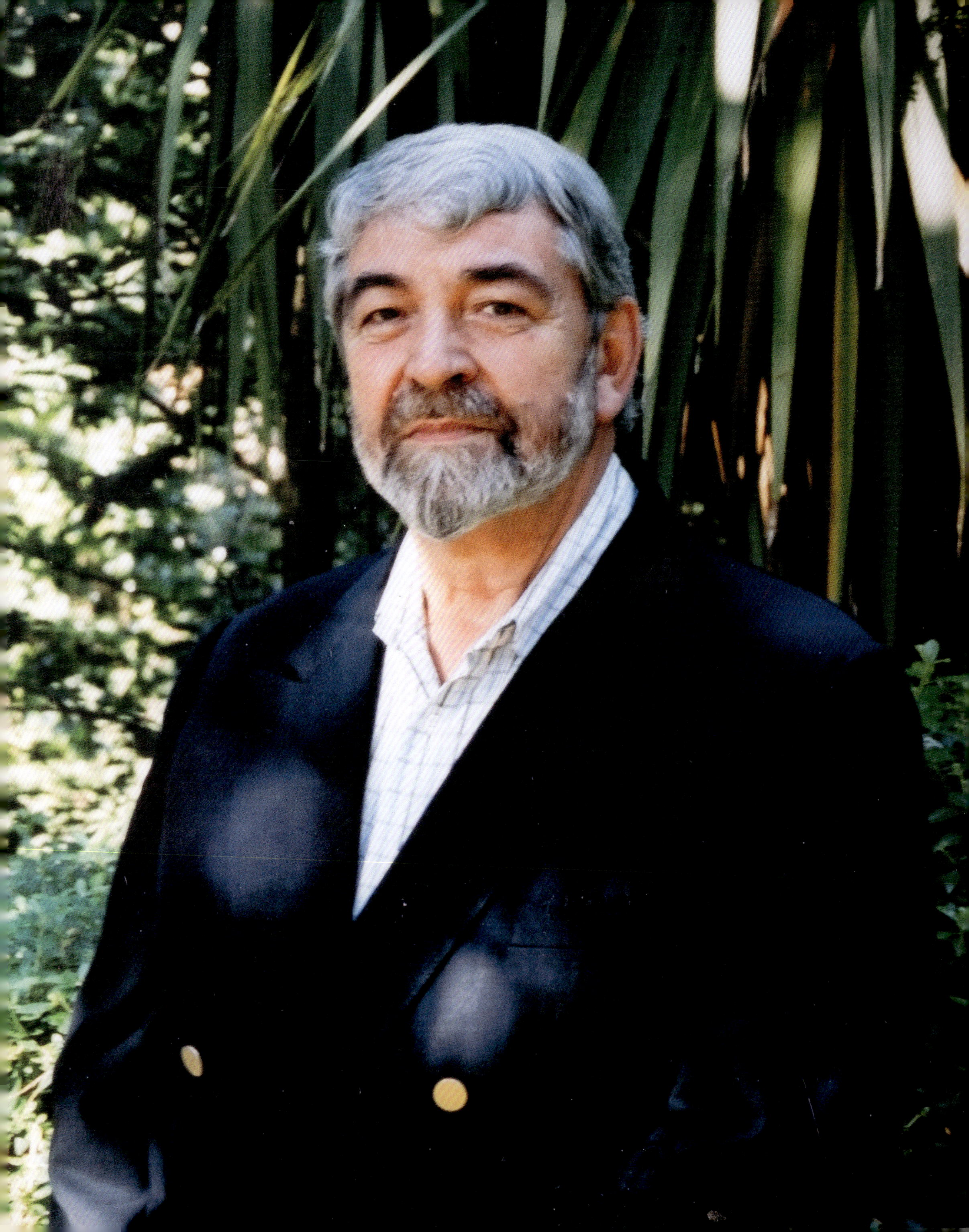

If high intelligence and an energetic, single minded pursuit of a goal might usually be thought to ensure success in business, then it is no surprise that John and Mary Goodyear built up their specialist consultancy company MBL (founded in 1965 shortly after graduating from UCL with a degree in Psychology and Anthropology) and within 30 years turned it into one of the biggest and most successful in the market research industry, with 26 offices in 17 countries.

If you add John Goodyear's creative flair for acquisition of great potential and natural eye for quality to his nascent hobby of 19th Century English watercolours, then it was also inevitable that he would go on to amass a significant and idiosyncratic collection during his lifetime.

When John and Mary sold their company MBL Group plc to a USA based public company in 1997 and fully retired in 2000, they turned to new and varied business opportunities whilst refining their hobbies and interests within a new social life in Guernsey, which became their home. The large and impressive Albert Goodwin and Hercules Brabazon Brabazon collections had a permanent home at last and hung happily amongst the Indian, Chinese, and South East Asian artworks – the beautiful spoils of a travelling man with a magpie eye.

I observed the early years of this obsessive hunt for the best watercolours as his increasing self-belief and sensual nature drew him closer to those artworks that gave him pleasure.

We had both attended an English watercolour sale at the Bond Street rooms of Phillips Auctioneers. It was the early 80s and late 19th Century pictures were beginning to get increased attention in the market place. Artists like Albert Goodwin, Hercules Brabazon Brabazon and Thomas Bush Hardy were being acquired by 'new money' – new buyers whom had come into collecting without the restrictions and rules of traditional prejudice. These buyers were backing their taste and judgement and so recreating a new age for Victorian art that echoed the surge of patronage amongst the new rich, industrialists and merchants of a century before.

So from different backgrounds two energetic, slightly driven young men in their late thirties came face to face and found they had spontaneously developed identical artistic predilections. This might be considered repetition but certainly there had never been any deviation or hesitation as we had independently and forcefully built our collections.

We were formally introduced by Hammond Smith, art lecturer and author of the biography of Albert Goodwin (Leigh-On-Sea: F Lewis, 1977). The memory lingers cheerfully and vividly in mind – John was six foot, slim, very handsome and already bristling with the warm and benign self confidence that I was to observe never left him in his leisure hours. On that day the first impression of a charismatic personality was embellished further by a dense but well-shaped Lebedevian beard, and then taken to another level of singularity by tight black leather trousers and a boldly striped Turnbull & Asser shirt. Ten years on, as the good life remodelled the shape of this *bon viveur*, 32 Turnbull & Asser shirts were to be gifted to me with John's characteristic generosity. As you ask, the trousers were never a possibility and have long since made their own way to a museum of their choosing.

To everyone's surprise we got on well and remained close friends through half a lifetime, enclosed rather than divided by our passion for the same artists. We were further bonded by a shared love of good company, good food and New World wines. John would later start up the Rowsley Fault Vineyard near Geelong, Australia, which continues to this day producing high quality wines.

I always remained the main conduit through which much of his English watercolour enthusiasm flowed, but John was an independent and bought widely from other dealers and in auction. He loved to talk about new prizes and did not look for approbation or instruction. No advice was asked for and none given.

During the early years of our friendship, John and Mary's empire building in the Far East precluded regular contact and I saw less of them. They were both voracious readers and John would return from a succession of long haul flights to intermittently enhance my life with didactic reading lists, which I still have, written in John's sedulous copper plate hand. So much of the modern British novel that I read today – William Boyd, Ian McEwan, Julian Barnes, Angus Wilson and

JOHN R GOODYEAR REMEMBERED

Paul Theroux, was engendered by them. Their happiness in sharing their cultural life extended to their love of opera and for 30 years they became significant patrons of Glyndebourne Festival Opera and regularly hosted friends and clients in their corporate seats during the season. I have always been content to paddle in the shallows of operatic enthusiasm and rarely joined them in the deep end of high opera. I was once invited to a particularly crepuscular and ponderous production of Don Giovanni. At a moment of great seriousness I got the giggles and even in the secluded dark of an opera box there was nowhere to hide. I wasn't asked back.

Weekends in their delightful thatched cottage 'Shrub End' in East Barton near Bury St Edmunds were much more in keeping with our mutual taste and I retain vibrant memories of evenings spent at bibulous dinner parties where the witty and effervescent Angus Wilson was a regular visitor.

This immersion in the life of East Anglia triggered off John's curiosity in its artistic heritage, so within a few years he had surrounded himself with artists of the Norwich School and a significant collection of watercolours by the amateur artist, John Constable patron and Woodbridge solicitor Thomas Churchyard.

John had a naturally robust constitution throughout his life until near the end, and all the excesses of a generous evening's entertaining were dispersed the next day with long and vigorous bouts of exercise. John and Mary were great walkers and as I contemplate the route marches through Thetford Forest I am visited by an ironic sadness in recollection, as I think of John's last years immured in a wheelchair by a rare and progressive neurological illness. His watercolour collection that surrounded him still gave him pleasure which he expressed enthusiastically if falteringly in his final days. These major collections of Albert Goodwin, Hercules Brabazon Brabazon and Early English watercolours remain as a symbol of his warmth, his curiosity, his intelligence and his all-pervading love of life.

Dr Chris Beetles, March 2022

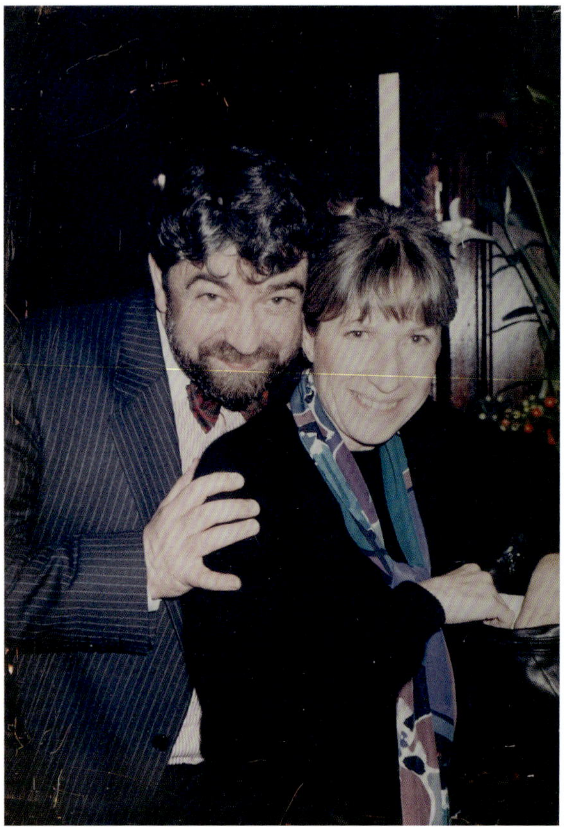

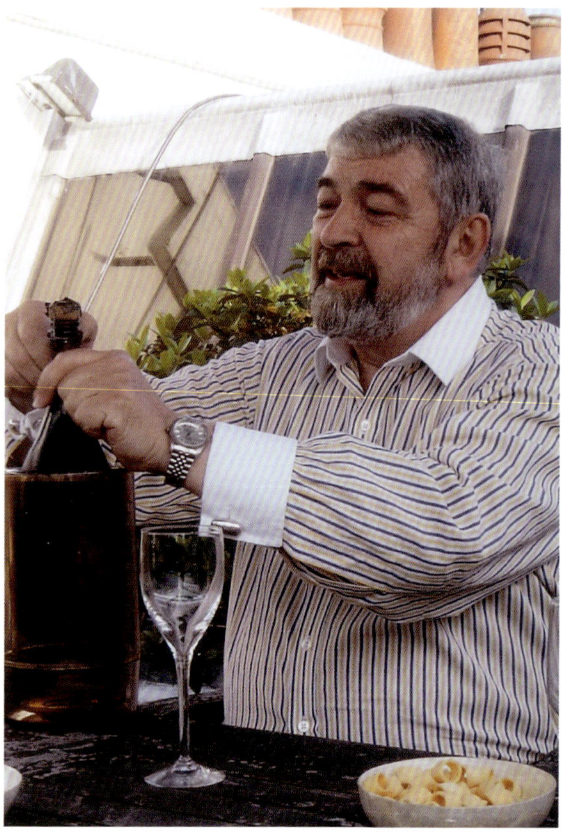

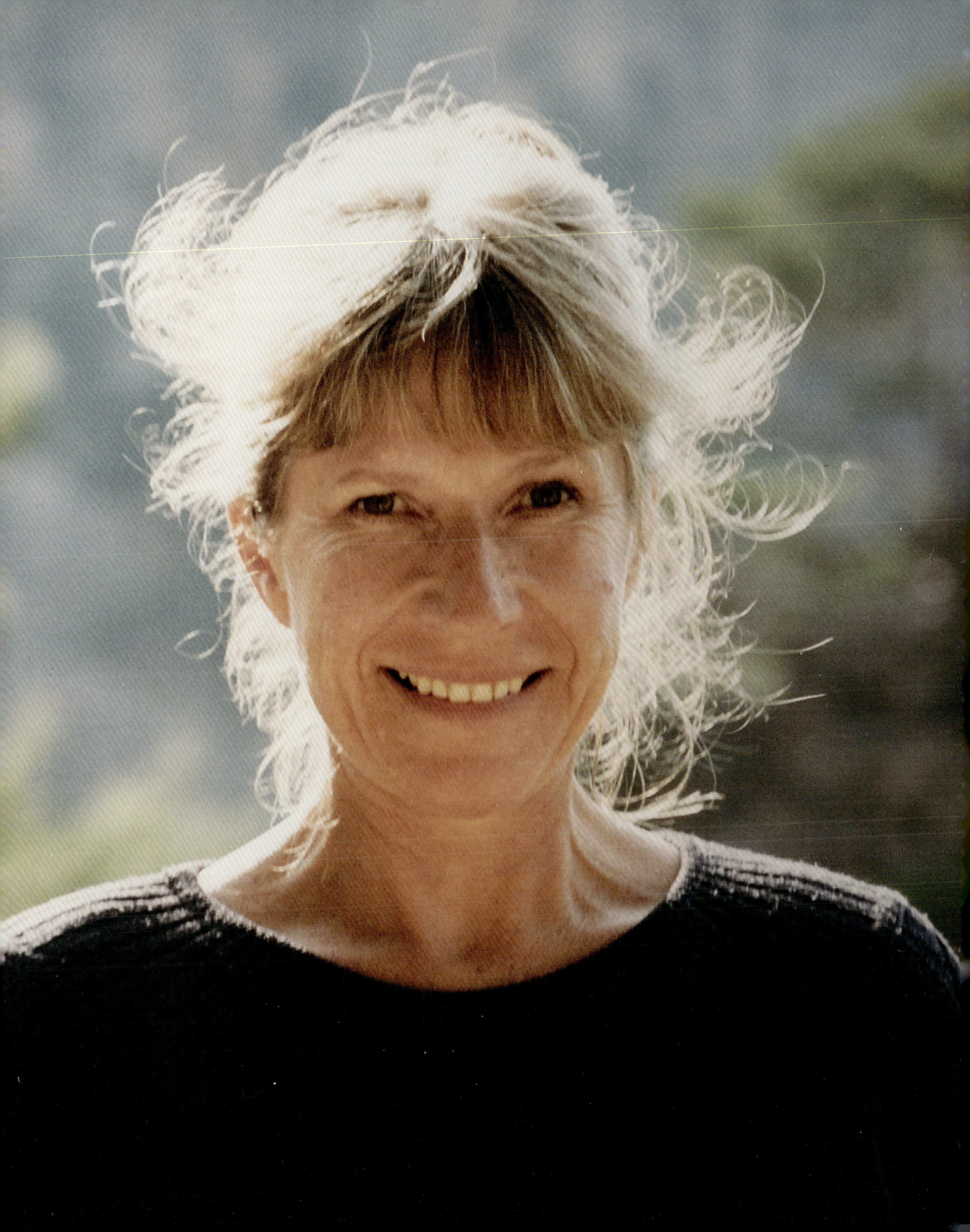

ALBERT GOODWIN RWS (1845-1932)
CHRONOLOGY OF LIFE AND WORK

17 January 1845
Albert Frederick Goodwin [AG] was born at 1 Acton Place, 62 Boxley Road, Maidstone, Kent, to the builder, Samuel Goodwin, and his wife, Rosetta (née Smith). He was the seventh of eight surviving children. The most artistically significant of his siblings were William (1833-1916), who had artistic talents but joined the Royal Engineers, Charles (1840-1907?), who became a wood carver and frame-maker, and Harry (1842-1925) and Frank (1848-1873), who became painters.

During his childhood, AG attended Mr William Henry Wicksteed's School at Rocky Hill House, Bedford Place, London Road, Maidstone. He and his family were General Baptists who worshipped at Bethel Chapel, Union Street. His father, who had built the chapel and its Sunday school in 1834, sometimes preached there, while his uncle, the organ builder, Thomas Goodwin, was its organist. According to Hammond Smith, 'Although quite delicate as a boy, Goodwin grew into a sturdy youth, noted for being a strong swimmer and a keen cyclist' (Hammond Smith, *Albert Goodwin RWS*, Leigh-on-Sea: F Lewis, 1977, page 13).

1851
The young sibling painters, Rosa (1829-1882) and John Brett (1831-1902), were living in Boxley Road, close to AG, and may have had an influence on his interest in art. Like him, they were drawn into the orbit of the Pre-Raphaelites.

By 1854
Hammond Smith has stated that, AG 'attracted the attention of the local printer, Mr Vince Hall, who, it seems, was acquainted with William Holman Hunt [1827-1910], one of the founder members of the Pre-Raphaelite Brotherhood' (Smith 1977, page 13). This is almost certainly the bookseller, John Vine Hall, who lived in Maidstone until 1854, and was an associate of AG's father.

1855
AG first exhibited (according to his obituary in *The Times*, 12 April 1932).

1855-60
During the late 1850s, AG began an apprenticeship with a draper. However, he stayed with him for just six months, and probably left to train as a painter. At some point, he met the Pre-Raphaelite painter, Arthur Hughes (1832-1915), who married in Maidstone in 1855, and lived in the town with his wife and children between 1858 and 1860. AG may have been introduced to Hughes by Holman Hunt, though he later stated that Hughes discovered him painting in a wood. Hughes became AG's first teacher, and AG painted one of Hughes's children. (Later, AG gave lessons in watercolour to Hughes's eldest child, Arthur Foord Hughes, in Lynmouth.)

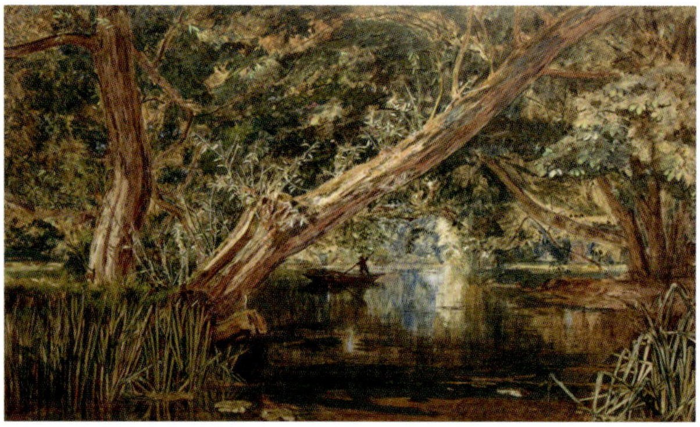

The Wooded Lake

1859
AG painted Bluebell Hill nr Maidstone, which he inscribed on reverse: '*Bluebell Hill nr Maidstone* painted when I was about 14 AD AG. But amended Feb 5th 1925 when past eighty!'

May-July 1860
AG first exhibited at the Royal Academy of Arts, London: no 156, *Under the Hedge* (oil).

Bluebell Hill nr Maidstone

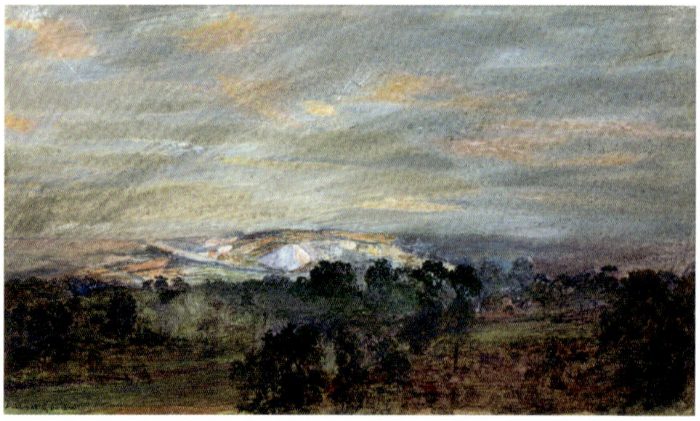

16 March 1863
AG's mother, Rosetta, died in Maidstone.

1863-1869
Hughes introduced AG to John Ruskin, who asked to see some of his drawings and then bought them; AG also gave Ruskin a lesson in watercolour painting. It has been generally thought that this occurred in 1869. However, according to Hughes's son, Arthur, it was as a result of Ruskin's payment of £50 that AG was able to spend five weeks in Hastings, as his first painting ground, and this trip took place in 1863. AG himself remembered that he 'had saved up five pounds and lived on it there for five weeks. Happily the old town remains a picturesque delight still' (catalogue to the Fine Art Society exhibition of March 1896).

Circa 1864-68
Hughes introduced AG to Ford Madox Brown (1821-1893), and he began to study under him in London. So he entered the circle of William Morris, D G Rossetti, William Bell Scott and George Price Boyce. According to his daughter, Olive, he 'worked in William Morris's firm in Red Lion Square for some time with his brother, Harry' (letter to Sidney Harris, 26 November 1931?).

1864
AG made his first visits overseas, going to Holland (including Rotterdam and Amsterdam) and, in the summer, Jersey.

September 1864
AG visited Newcastle where he had planned to see the industrialist and collector, James Leathart, both Hughes and Brown having recommended AG to him. In the event, he was apparently too shy to visit him, though he did make contact with the painters, Scott and Boyce, and may have been travelling with the latter. He returned from Newcastle with a 'host of material for delineating the Tyne and all things in her neighbourhood' (as he stated in a letter dated 20 September 1864). During this trip, he also visited Durham and Whitby. Leathart eventually owned at least five of his watercolours, four dating to 1864, including *St Anthony's Works, Newcastle upon Tyne*, which depicts the smelting works of the lead manufacturers Locke, Blackett & Co, which were extended in 1864, and came under the direction of Leathart as managing partner.

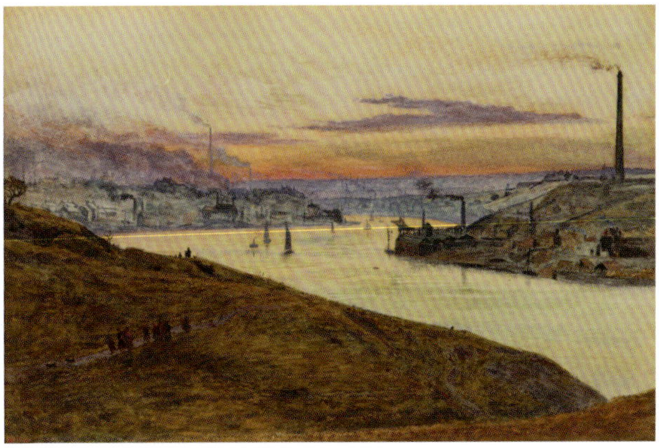

St Anthony's Works, Newcastle upon Tyne

Spring 1865
AG visited Bideford, on what was possibly his first trip to Devon.

1866
AG exhibited at the Dudley Gallery, Egyptian Hall, Piccadilly, London, for the first time, and his contributions were praised by *The Spectator*.

16 February 1867
AG married Mary Ann Lucas, aged about 27, the eldest daughter of George Lucas, a Brighton fruiterer, at St Nicholas's Church, Arundel. They lived initially at The Parade, Arundel.

1868
AG and his wife, Mary Ann, were living at 10 Waterloo Street, Brighton.

May-July 1868
AG's brother, Harry, exhibited at the Royal Academy for the first time.

29 June 1868
AG's brother, Harry, married Henrietta Lucas, the sister of AG's wife, Mary Ann, in Brighton.

13 December 1869
AG's first wife, Mary Ann, died, aged 30, of tubercular peritonitis.

Circa 1869
AG joined Arthur Hughes and his family at 2 Finborough Road, West Brompton, London, and became the artist's studio assistant, working chiefly on large monochrome paintings for Manchester, including *The Central Executive Cot-*

ton Famine Relief Committee (Manchester Town Hall). He continued to use 2 Finborough Road as his studio address until 1877.

Before January 1871
AG visited Bruges.

1871
AG was elected an Associate of the Society of Painters in Water Colours. (This would become the Royal Society of Painters in Water-Colours in 1881.)

2 April 1871
According to the Census, AG was living at Maltravers Street, Arundel, Sussex, with his brother, Harry, who is described as a 'Professor of Music', and Harry's wife, Henrietta. However, Henrietta died later the same year.

Spring 1871
Ruskin wrote to AG inviting him to work with him at Abingdon, near Oxford, 'before we start for Verona', suggesting that they had planned a trip to Italy. AG joined Ruskin at the Crown & Thistle, Abingdon, producing drawings for Ruskin (two views for the Rudimentary Series of the Ruskin Art Collection in the Ashmolean Museum, Oxford).

May-July 1871
AG exhibited *The Medway at Maidstone* at the Royal Academy.

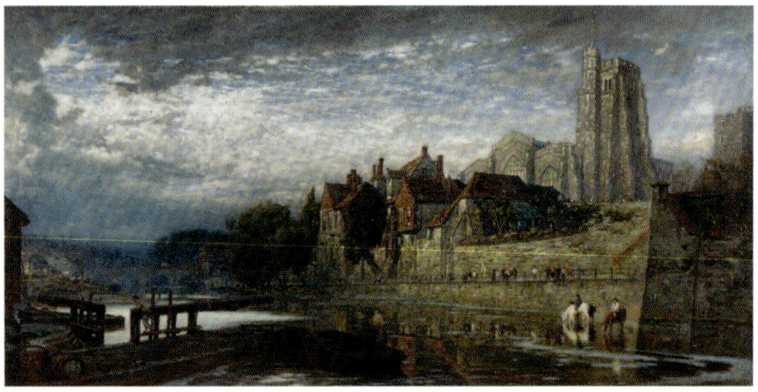

The Medway at Maidstone

July 1871
AG stayed with John Ruskin and Arthur and Joan Severn at the New Bath Hotel, Matlock Bath, in the Peak District. Though Ruskin was seriously ill, he 'made Goodwin and [Severn] go and explore all the interesting mines and caverns in the neighbourhood' (James Dearden (ed), *The Professor: Arthur Severn's Memoir of John Ruskin*, London: George Allen & Unwin, 1967, page 44)

1872
AG's brother, Harry, married fellow painter, Kate Malleson, in Croydon.

April-July 1872
AG travelled with Ruskin in Europe (and especially Italy and Switzerland).

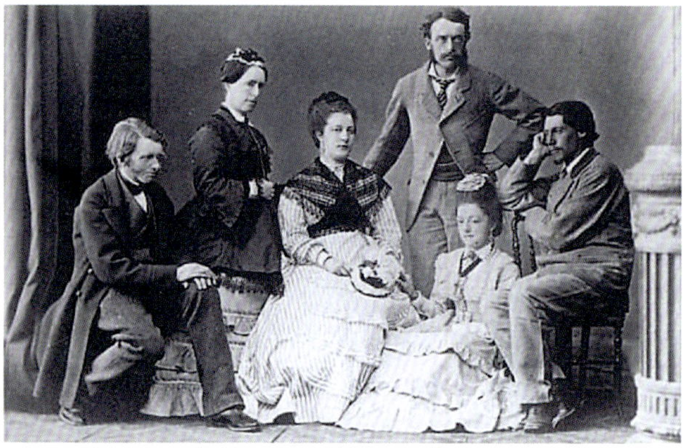

Albert Goodwin with John Ruskin in Italy in 1872
Left to right: John Ruskin, Mrs J C Hilliard, Mrs Joan Severn, Arthur Severn, Constance Hilliard, Albert Goodwin

1873
AG went to Switzerland, staying three months in the village of Simplon.

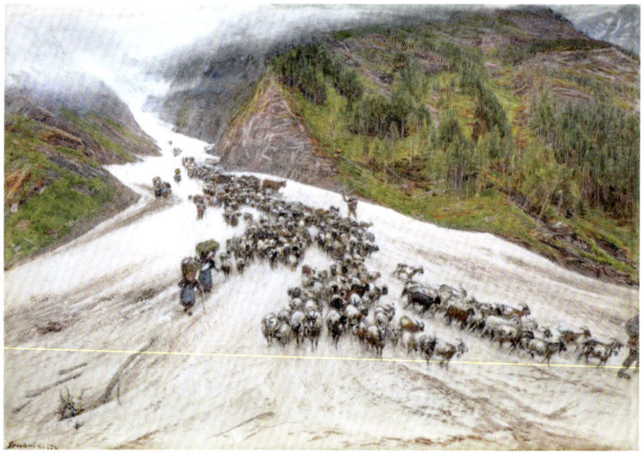

The Goat-Herd in the Swiss Alps [4]

15 April 1873
AG married his second wife, Alice Desborough, aged 23, at Holy Trinity, Gidleigh, Devon. She was the daughter of Henry Desborough, formerly the Secretary to the Atlas Fire & Life Assurance Company, who had retired to Devon and died in 1862. She and AG would have seven children.

13 September 1873
AG's brother, Frank, died in Maidstone.

2 February 1874
AG's daughter, Ivy, was born in Hastings, Sussex.

1876
AG and his wife, Alice, travelled to Egypt, via Marseilles, Naples, Gibraltar and Crete.

29 December 1876
AG's sister, Marianne (known as Polly), died in Maidstone.

1877
AG, with his wife and daughter, moved from London to 7 Montpelier Terrace, Ilfracombe, Devon. AG visited Lucerne, Switzerland, in the same year.

25 November 1877
AG's father, Samuel, died in Maidstone.

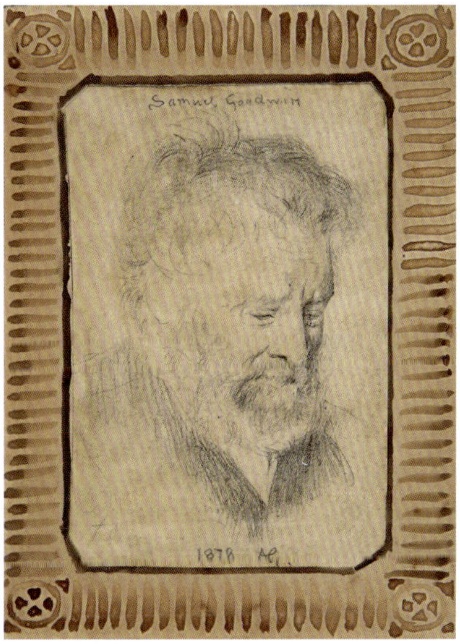

Samuel Goodwin

19 May 1879
AG and his family visited Arthur Hughes in London.

August 1879
Maidstone Museum held 'A Loan Exhibition of pictures by Mr Albert Goodwin, Mr and Mrs Harry Goodwin, the late Mr Frank Goodwin, Mr W Sydney Goodwin, and Mrs F E Green (née Goodwin)'.

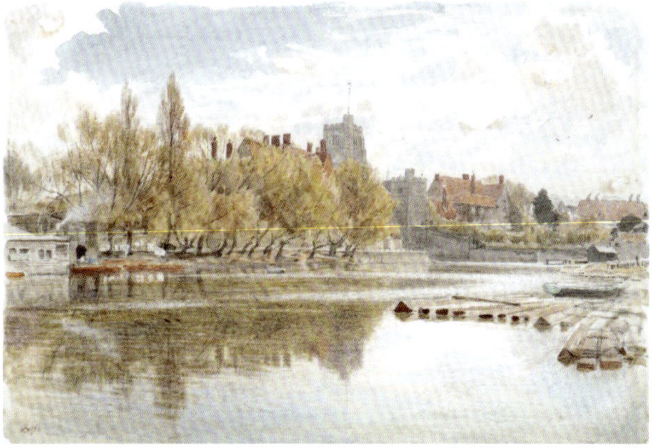

Maidstone [7]

Easter 1880
AG visited Holland and Belgium, including Dordrecht, Bruges and Ypres.

Summer 1880
AG visited Charles Darwin at Down House, and produced two watercolours of its exterior. (In 1876, Darwin had purchased AG's *The Old Walls of Winchester*, from the Society of Painters in Water Colours.)

21 August 1880
AG's daughter, Olive, was born in Hastings, Sussex.

1881
AG was elected a member of the Royal Society of Painters in Water-Colours.

3 April 1881
According to the Census, AG was staying at Ferndale House, Lynmouth, Devon, as a 'boarder' with Maria Berriman, and is described as 'a landscape painter'. With him are Alice and their daughters, Ivy and Olive, and Alice Ann Herswell, a 15-year-old nurse/domestic servant from Barnstaple.

6 September 1881
AG's daughter, Edytha Margaret, was born in Hastings.

12 August 1883
The date of the first entry of AG's diary (as privately published in 1934).

26 December 1884
AG's son, Arthur Albert Desborough, known initially as Albert and later as Desborough, was born in Ilfracombe.

May 1886
AG held his first exhibition at the Fine Art Society, London, 'A Collection of Drawings in City, Town and Hamlet by Albert Goodwin RWS'.

23 July 1886
AG's daughter, Christabel, was born in Ilfracombe, Devon.

1887
AG visited Lucerne and the Italian Lakes with his brother, Harry.

September 1887
Arthur Hughes visited AG in Ilfracombe.

1888
AG accompanied Ruskin and Severn on a tour of Northern France that included Abbeville.

28 March 1888
AG's daughter, Alice Desborough, was born in Ilfracombe.

1889
AG visited Arthur Hughes in London.

June 1890
AG visited Locarno.

28 July 1890
AG's son, Harold Desborough Goodwin, was born in Ilfracombe.

December 1890
The Fine Art Society held the exhibition, 'A Collection of Water-Colour Drawings of Many-Sided Nature by Albert Goodwin, RWS'.

5 April 1891
According to the Census, AG was boarding at 15 West Pier, Whitby, Yorkshire, with the iron shipwright, James Welsh, and his family. AG's wife, Alice, was living at 7 Montpelier Terrace, Ilfracombe, the 'living in husband's profession'. With her are their seven children – Ivy, Olive, Edytha, Albert, Christabel, Alice and Harold – and two servants: Sarah A Delbridge, a 26-year-old cook, and Mary A Beer, a 22-year-old nurse. Alice's mother and sister, Mary, were living at 3 Montpelier Terrace.

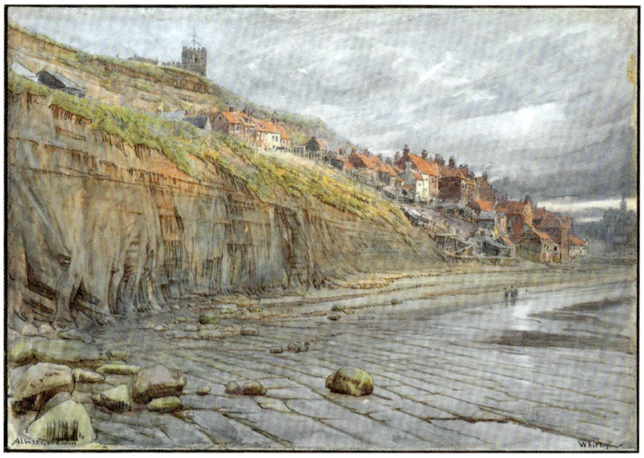

Whitby [12]

March 1891
AG visited Whitby.

1892
AG visited Norway, including Bergen.

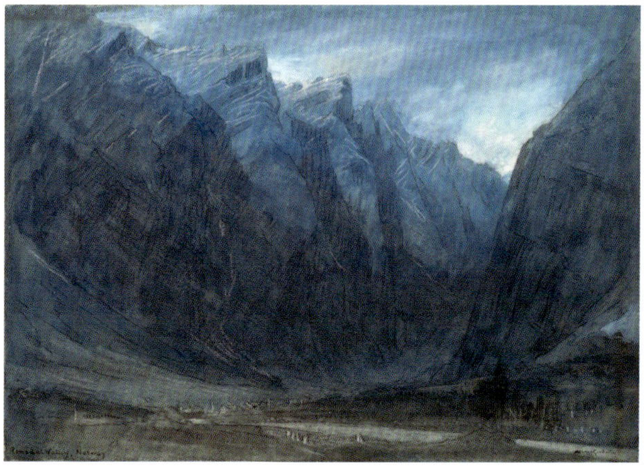

Romsdal Valley, Norway [28]

October 1893
The Fine Art Society held the exhibition, 'A Collection of Paintings and Drawings by Albert Goodwin, RWS'.

12 April 1894
AG's mother-in-law, Mary Desborough, died at 3 Montpelier Terrace, Ilfracombe.

1895
AG went to India, as a result of 'the kindness of my friend, Dr G B Longstaff, who both persuaded me to go and made the way thereto easy' (catalogue to the exhibition held at the Fine Art Society in March 1896). George Blundell Longstaff was a prominent lepidopterist and statistician.

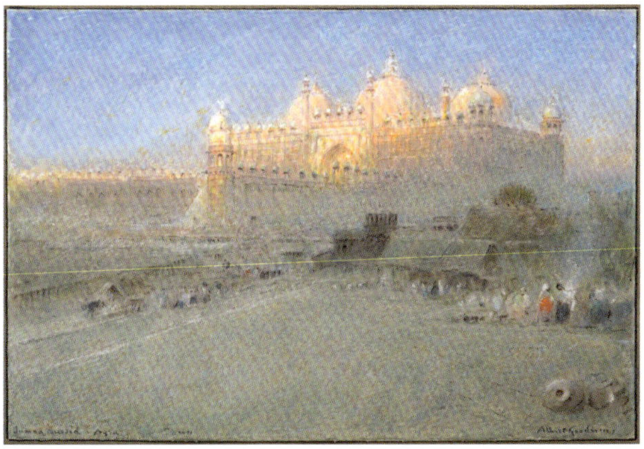

Jumna Musjid, Agra, Dawn [22]

March 1896
The Fine Art Society held the exhibition, 'A Collection of Pictures and Drawings of Imaginative Landscape in Europe and Asia by Albert Goodwin, RWS'.

8 November 1898
AG's daughter, Ivy, married Norman Bruce Elliott, a doctor from Lambeth, London. (They had a son, Ian Desborough Elliott, born on 9 September 1901.)

December 1898
The Fine Art Society held the exhibition, 'Pictures and Sketches including a series of Whitby, and "The First Christmas Dawn", by Albert Goodwin'.

Before 1900
AG almost joined the Salvation Army (as he mentioned in his diary on 10 July 1900).

March 1900
AG went to Southern Italy including Naples, Pompeii and Torre del Greco.

Taormina [32]

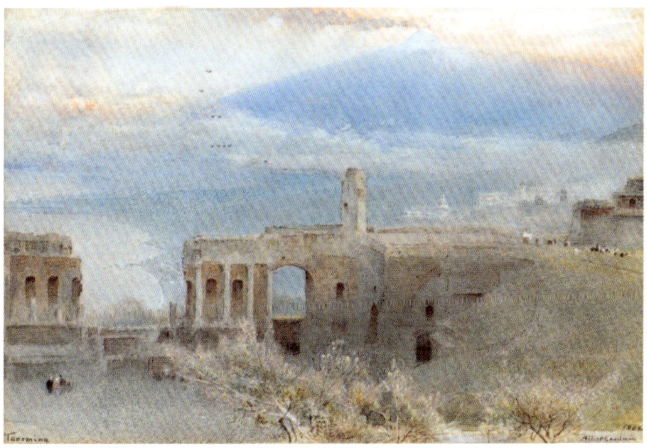

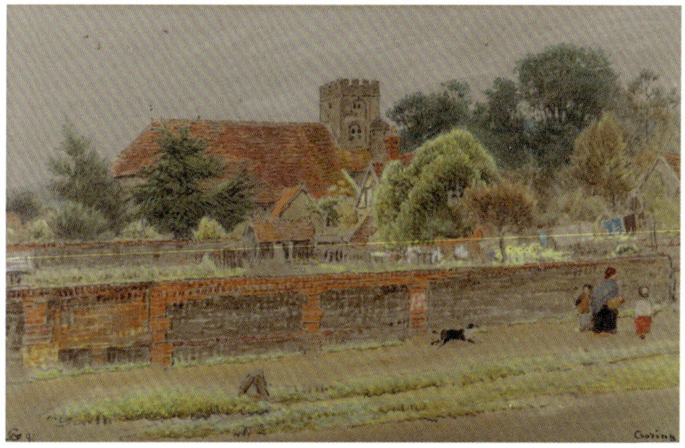

Goring [10]

July 1900
AG visited Oxford, Goring and Windsor.

November 1900
The Fine Art Society held 'An Exhibition of Pictures and Watercolours entitled "In Praise of All The Churches" by Albert Goodwin, RWS'.

1901
AG's sister, Emma Hobday, died.

31 March 1901
According to the Census, AG was staying at the home of his friend, Dr Longstaff, Twitchen House, Mortehoe, Devon. With him were Alice and their four younger daughters, Olive, Edytha, Christabel and Alice. Their two sons were at boarding schools.

1902
Robert Dunthorne's The Rembrandt Gallery, London held the exhibition, 'Sunset and Colour from East and West. Drawings by Albert Goodwin, RWS'.

January-May 1902
AG left the Isle of Wight for Barbados, accompanied by his daughter, Edytha. He travelled aboard the WIMS Trent, as a guest of Arthur McConnell, the husband of Alice's niece, Emily. McConnell worked for Booker Brothers, McConnell and Co, general merchants, owners of plantations and shippers. Arriving at their destination on 2 February, the Goodwins parted with McConnell and boarded the RMS Eden, journeying to St Vincent, Grenada, Trinidad and Jamaica. They arrived in Philadelphia on 14 April, and went to Niagara by train the following day. They then spent three nights in New York between 26 and 29 April, and returned to England on 7 May.

1904
Robert Dunthorne's The Rembrandt Gallery, London, held the exhibition, 'Water Colour Drawings by Albert Goodwin, RWS'.

May 1905
The Fine Art Society held 'An Exhibition of Water-Colours of the Cathedrals of England by Albert Goodwin, RWS'.

1906
AG and his wife moved to 'Ellerslie', Bexhill-on-Sea, Sussex, with their five single children.

May 1906
The Turner House, Penarth, Wales, held an 'Exhibition of Works by Albert Goodwin, RWS' (alongside sculpture by W Goscombe John).

1907
AG went to Lucerne, Switzerland. His brother, Charles, may have died in the same year.

January 1907
The Fine Art Society held 'An Exhibition of Water-Colours of Dawn and Sunset by Albert Goodwin, RWS'.

May-August 1907
AG's daughter, Edytha, exhibited at the Royal Academy for the first of four times.

1908
The Leggatt Brothers Gallery, London, held the exhibition, 'Drawings and Pictures by Albert Goodwin, RWS'.

March 1908
AG's son, Arthur Albert Desborough, married Evelyn Saunders in Hailsham, Sussex.

January-March 1909
AG went – via the Spanish coast, Naples and Vesuvius – to Egypt, staying in Cairo and Suez.

April-June 1909
AG went to Italy and Switzerland with his wife and two of their daughters, visiting Baveno, Lago Maggiore, Fribourg, Berne, Lucerne and Engelberg.

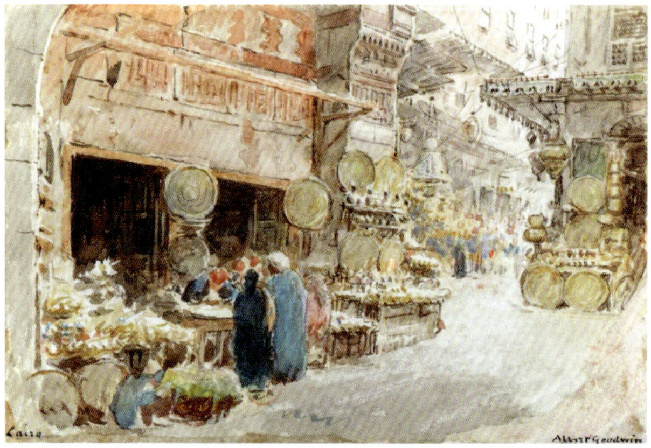

Cairo [37]

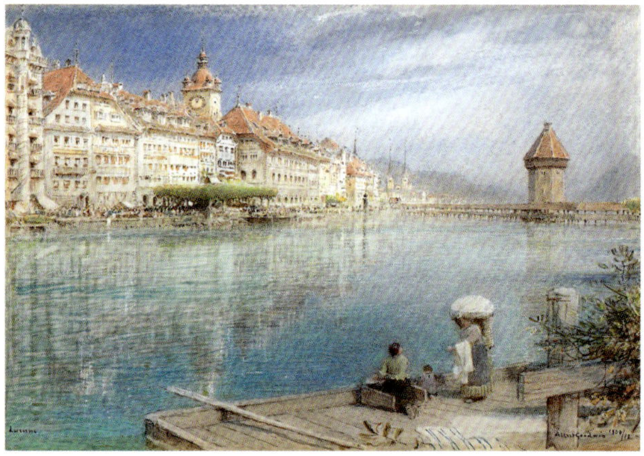

Lucerne [42]

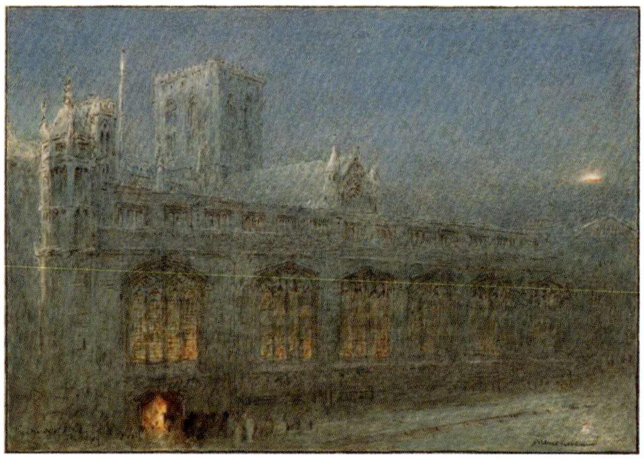

The Church of the Belfry, York [33]

July-September 1909
AG and his wife visited Whitby, Edinburgh, York and Weybourne, Norfolk.

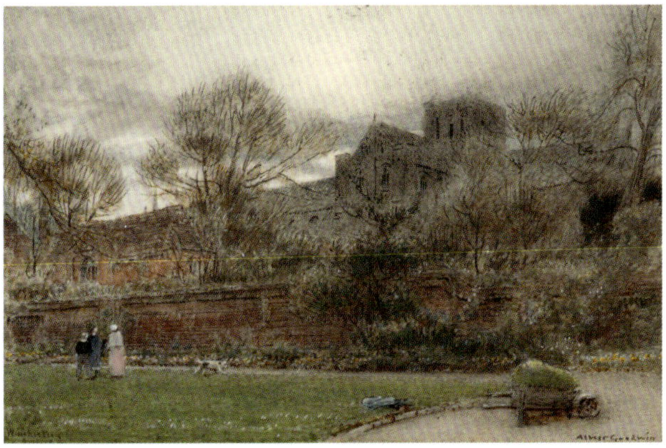

Winchester [40]

October 1909
AG visited Bath and Winchester, the latter as a guest of Montague Rendall, the Headmaster of Winchester College, 'a sort of cousin of my wife's' (Diary, 28 October 1909).

Circa 1910
Edytha painted a watercolour miniature on ivory of AG [below right].

4 January 1910
Arthur Hughes and his son, Godfrey, visited AG.

March 1910
A Lys Baldry's article, 'The Art of Mr Albert Goodwin, RWS', was published in *The Studio*, March 1910, pages 86-97.

August 1910
AG went to Switzerland (with his wife, children and Ivy's two children), visiting Lauterbrunnen and Spiez, Lake Thun.

September 1910
AG visited Windsor.

February 1911
AG visited Edinburgh and Scarborough with his wife and daughter, Christabel, and also Daisy (possibly his great niece).

April 1911
AG considered emigrating to New Zealand.

2 April 1911
According to the Census, AG was living at 'Ellerslie', Bexhill-on-Sea, with his wife, Alice, and their five unmarried children: Olive, Edytha, Christabel, Alice and Harold.

May 1911
AG went to Switzerland with his wife and daughter, Edytha, visiting Weggis, Lake Lucerne and Engelberg.

July 1911
AG made visits to Cambridge and Windsor.

1912
The Leggatt Brothers Gallery held the exhibition, 'Water-Colour Drawings and Paintings by Albert Goodwin, RWS'.

January-April 1912
AG made his second visit to the West Indies as a guest of Arthur McConnell. He was accompanied by his daughter, Alice. They stayed at Barbados, Trinidad, Venezuela, Grenada, St Lucia, Martinique, St Kitts and Georgetown (Demerara, British Guiana). On 16 April, all three arrived in New York. Late in the month, they returned to England on the Mauretania.

1913
AG's sister, Rosetta Turner, died.

March 1913
AG's daughter, Edytha, married Ralph Longstaff in Battle, Sussex. (They lived at 'Twitchen', Mortehoe, Devon, and had 5 children between 1913 and 1924.)

Edytha Goodwin, *Albert Goodwin*

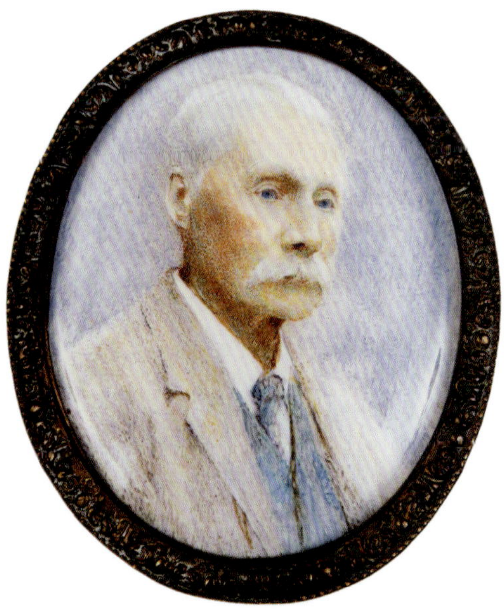

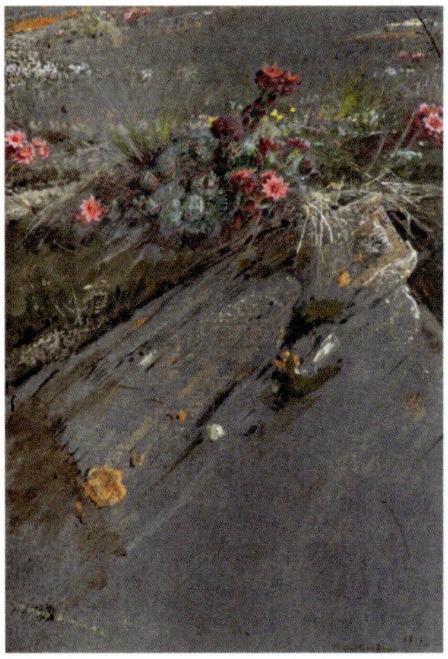

Stonecrop, Bumina Alp, Pontresina July 1913 [45]

June-July 1913
AG and his wife went to Switzerland, and visited Pontresina and Schaffhausen.

Summer 1913
AG took Kenneth Clark sketching.

Autumn 1913
AG probably visited Cashel, Tipperary.

October-November 1913
AG and his wife visited Cambridge and Norfolk.

January 1914
AG and his daughter, Olive, stayed in Penzance and made 'a very pleasant visit to Stanhope Forbes at Newlyn' (Diary, 18 January 1914); he then visited London where he called on Arthur Hughes.

February 1914
AG visited his daughter and son-in-law, Edytha and Ralph Longstaff, in Mortehoe, near Ilfracombe, returning there for the first time in almost 10 years.

May 1914
AG went to Italy, visiting Naples, Palermo and Taormina.

Summer 1914
AG took Kenneth Clark sketching.

June-July 1914
AG and his wife went to Switzerland, visiting Geneva and Chamonix.

September 1915
AG stayed in Chichester, and visited Bosham and Arundel.

December 1915
AG's brother, William Sydney, and his teacher, Arthur Hughes, both died in this month.

11 January 1916
AG's second wife, Alice, died. Soon after, he and his unmarried daughters built 'Little Ellerslie' in a field adjoining 'Ellerslie' and moved into that.

1 July 1916
AG's son, Harold, of the Middlesex Regiment, died in the Battle of the Somme.

October 1916
Walker's Galleries, London, mounted a memorial exhibition of the work of Arthur Hughes, AG providing the preface to the accompanying catalogue.

November 1916-1917
AG sailed – via South Africa – to Australia and New Zealand, visiting his son, Arthur Albert Desborough, in the latter, where he was working as a surveyor.

1917
AG went to Sicily with the shipping magnate, Sir Thomas Devitt.

April 1918
Sir Frederick Wedmore's article, 'Albert Goodwin, RWS', was published in *The Studio*, April 1918, pages 79-90.

May-June 1918
AG visited Bosham.

July-September 1918.
AG made two visits to Devon that included stays in Clovelly.

1919
The Leggatt Brothers Gallery held the exhibition, 'Drawings and Pictures by Albert Goodwin, RWS'.

By 1920
AG was elected to the membership of the Royal West of England Academy.

1920
The Collector's Gallery, London, held 'An Exhibition of Works by Albert Goodwin RWS'.

1921
Frost & Reed, Bristol, held the exhibition, 'Water-colours by Albert Goodwin RWS'.

1922
The Leggatt Brothers Gallery held the exhibition, 'Drawings and Pictures by Albert Goodwin, RWS'.

1925
AG's brother, Harry, died in Hastings.

March 1925
Vicar Brothers, London, held the exhibition, 'Water-Colour Drawings and Oil Paintings by Albert Goodwin, RWS'.

December 1925
The Municipal Art Gallery and Museum, Wolverhampton, held 'An Exhibition of Oil Paintings, Water Colour Drawings, Etc by Albert Goodwin, RWS RWA. Loaned by M B Walker, RWA Esq'.

1926
The City of Birmingham Museum and Art Gallery held 'A Collection of Oil Paintings, Water Colour Drawings etc by Albert Goodwin, RWS RWA. Lent by M B Walker Esq'.

1927
Walker Art Gallery, Liverpool, held an 'Exhibition of Pictures in Oil and Watercolour, by Albert Goodwin, RWS, lent by Matthew Biggar Walker, Esq, Wolverhampton'.

8 July 1927
The date of the last entry of AG's diary (as privately published in 1934).

9 March 1928
Messrs Christie, Manson & Woods, London, held the sale, 'A Collection of Works by Albert Goodwin, RWS RWA. The Property of Matthew Biggar Walker, Esq of 1 Park Crescent, Wolverhampton'.

25 July 1928
Lyndon Goodwin Harris was born in Halesowen, Worcestershire, to Sidney and Polly Harris, friends of AG and collectors of his work.

10 April 1932
AG died at 'Little Ellerslie', Bexhill-on-Sea, at the age of 87.

Detail of *Norwich* [8]

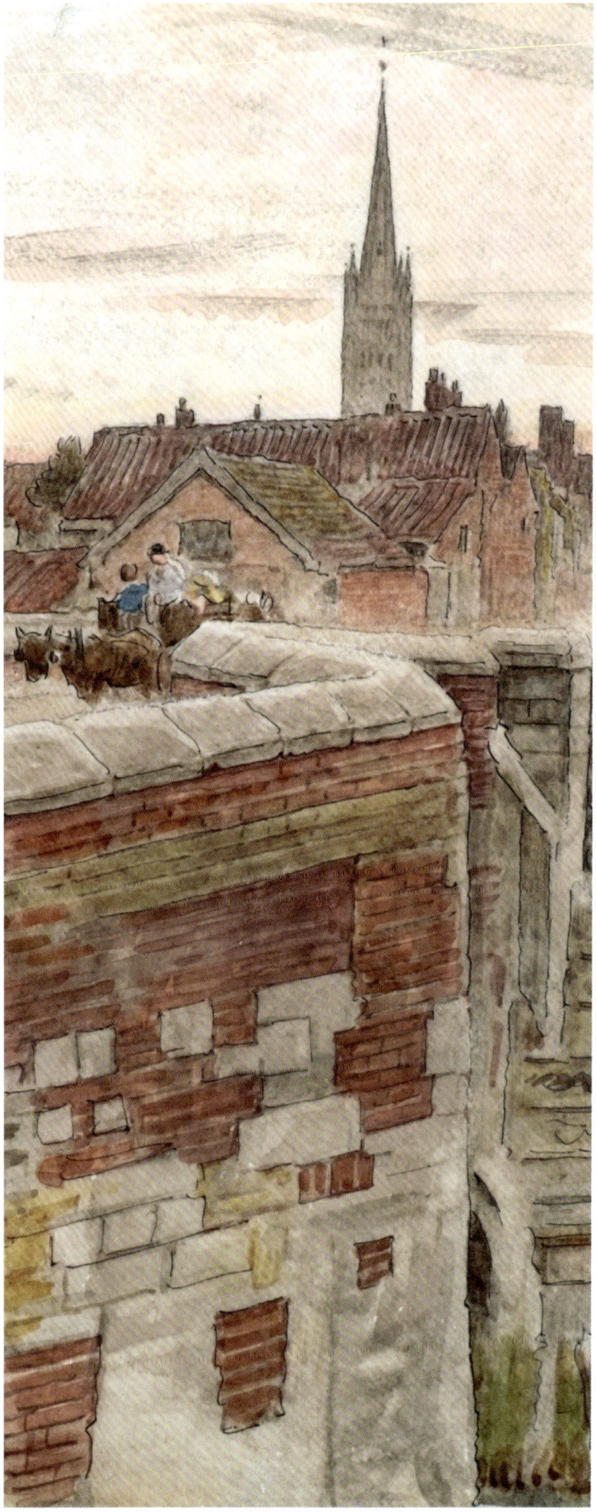

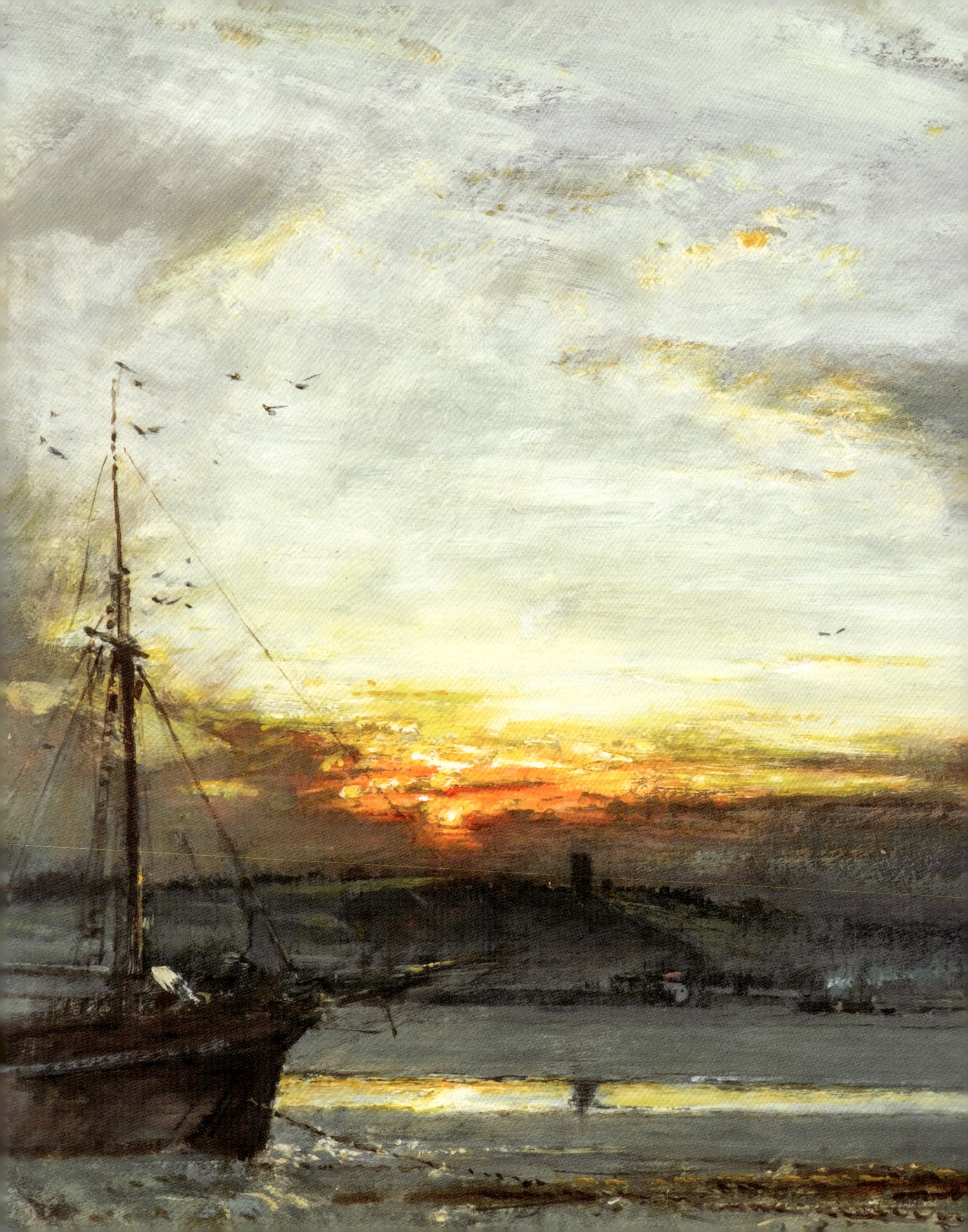

The John & Mary Goodyear Collection

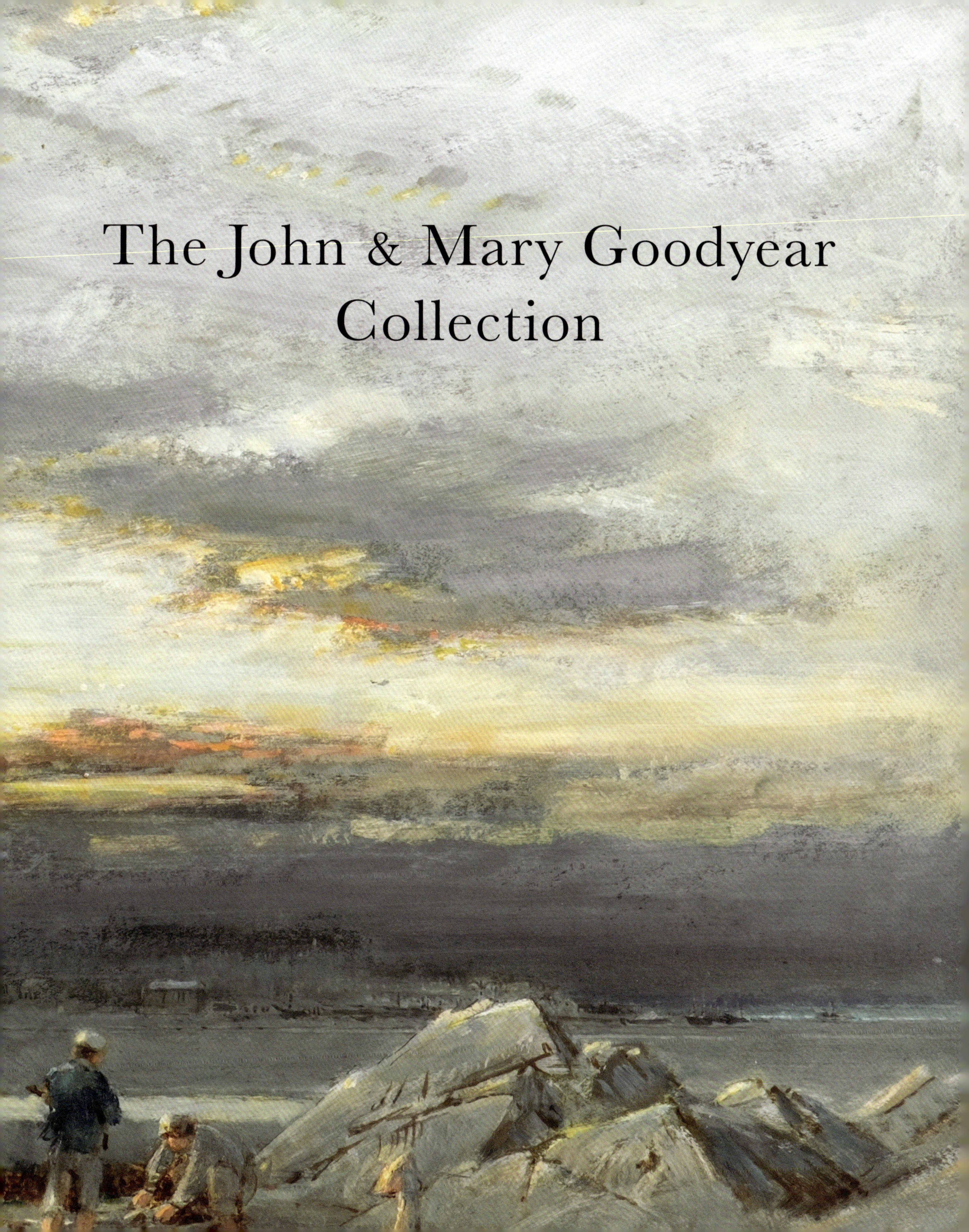

'But Ruskin's strong point never was colour. He was a safe guide in all matters of form or sentiment, but as to any interest in tone-values or greys "he cared for none of these things." Grey was to him always hateful, and I used to think what a lot of enjoyment he lost in this being blind to it in Nature, especially as Nature is so full of it, and it holds so useful a place in its economy. It was this feeling that made him look at Whistler's work with the contempt he did, and doubtless prompted the criticism which led to the law suit for libel that Whistler brought against him.'

(*The Diary of Albert Goodwin, RWS, 1883-1927*, Privately Printed, 1934, Page 105, 17 March 1909)

'The commonplace looked quite splendid, showing one how, given the right conditions, a view which would be without beauty or interest under one phase, might under another, and one that suited it, be perfectly beautiful. Ruskin did not enough agree with the great fact, Whistler too much. Ruskin's idea of a subject was apart from treatment, Whistler was that treatment was everything, subject didn't matter. But I think (though the truth lies between) Ruskin was the truer wisdom. Art ought to choose a subject which is beautiful in itself. Thereby it gets an inspiration and ought to be able to add all the addition that rightful treatment can add to its own intrinsic perfections. But Whistler would make out that a squalid ugly reach of the most uninteresting part of the Thames was just as good for the painter as the most intrinsically beautiful scene, colour justifying all things. So it does to some extent, but colour isn't everything.'

(*The Diary of Albert Goodwin, RWS, 1883-1927*, Privately Printed, 1934, Page 279, 29 December 1914)

1 **Fog on the River, Cheyney Walk, Chelsea**
Signed, inscribed with title and dated 'about 1862'
Watercolour with ink
10 ¼ x 14 inches
Literature:
Albert Goodwin RWS, 1845-1932, London: Chris Beetles Ltd, 1986, Limited Edition of 1000, Plate 3
Exhibited:
'Albert Goodwin RWS 1845-1932. 129 of His Best Works Borrowed From Private Collections',
a Museum Tour of the Royal Watercolour Society, Sheffield Mappin Art Gallery, Ruskin Gallery,
Stoke on Trent City Museum and Art Gallery, May-October 1986, No 3

This watercolour is not only a fascinating and early example of Goodwin's problem with spelling, it also demonstrates well the previously understated effect that Whistler's subject matter and treatment had on him. There are many references to Whistler in his writing all expressed with an appropriate muted enthusiasm; a typically even handed assessment, with recognition of Whistler's talent despite Goodwin's disapproval of dandified arrogance and secularism.

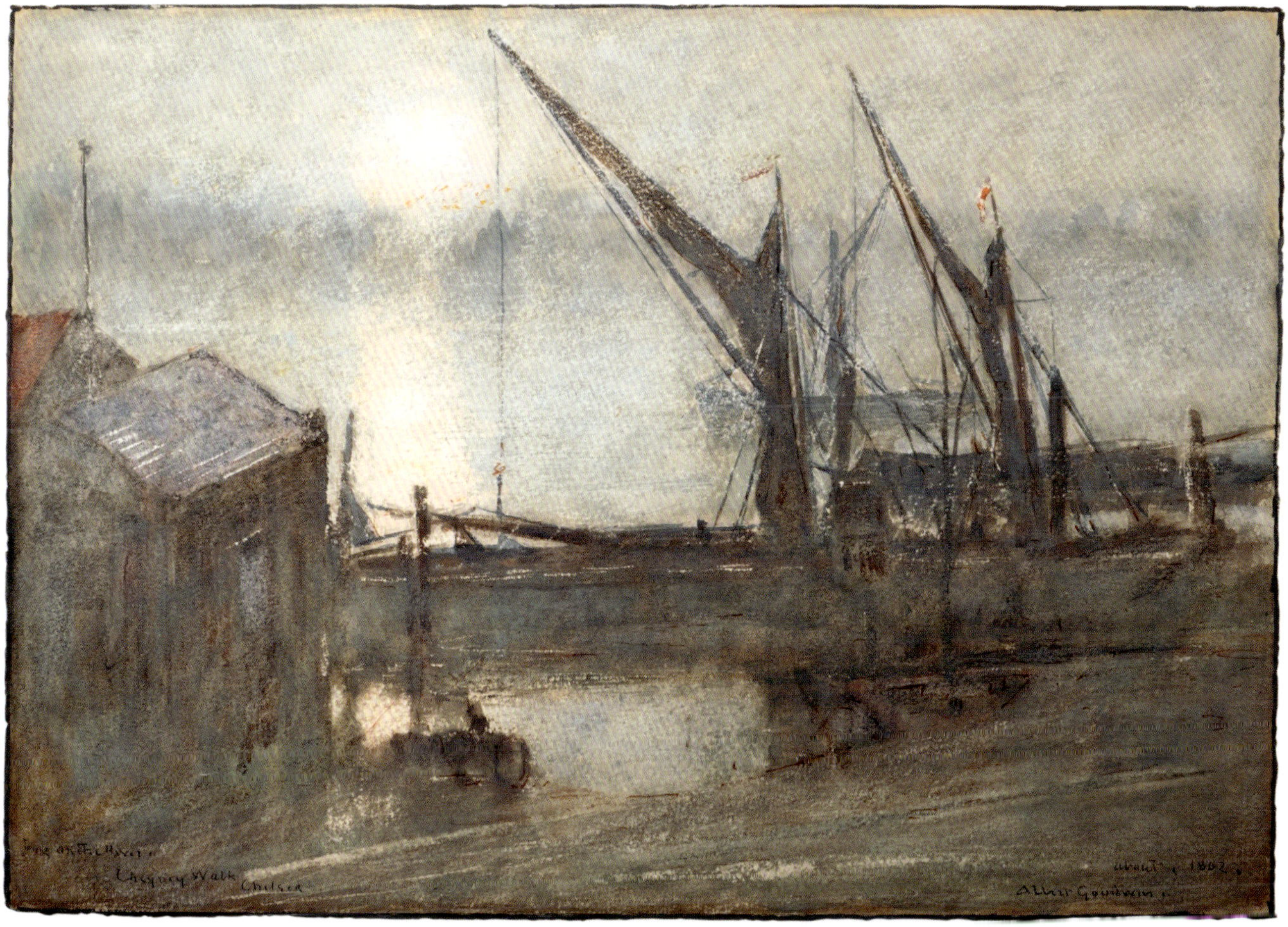
Walk
Chelsea
Albert Goodwin

'Revolution in Germany. Kiel and Hamburg in the hands of revolutionaries.
Kaiser's brother, Prince Henry, escapes disguised.
*These are some of the headings of to-night's "*Evening Standard*":*
"Delegates' hasty journey to Paris to sign Armistice."
"Perilous position of German Army."
Altogether I am reminded of the happenings which happened in France at the time I was the quest of Ruskin at the Crown and Thistle in Abingdon, when the news that came day by day was that which described the later stages of the Siege of Paris. The Commune, the pulling down of the Vendôme Columns and the burning of the Tuileries! That time was exciting enough, but this is a thousand times more so.'

(*The Diary of Albert Goodwin, RWS, 1883-1927*, Privately Printed, 1934, Page 436, 8 November 1918)

2 **The Road to "Glory"**
Signed, inscribed with title and dated 1870
Watercolour with bodycolour
19 ¼ x 24 ½ inches
Literature:
Hammond Smith, *Albert Goodwin RWS*, Leigh-on-Sea: F Lewis, 1977, Plate 5;
Albert Goodwin RWS, 1845-1932, London: Chris Beetles Ltd, 1986, Limited Edition of 1000, Plate 8
Exhibited:
'Albert Goodwin RWS 1845-1932', Bolton Museum and Art Gallery, August-September 1981, and touring to Canterbury, Newcastle upon Tyne, Leicester and Sotheby's Belgravia, 1981-82, No 57;
'Albert Goodwin RWS 1845-1932. 129 of His Best Works Borrowed From Private Collections', a Museum Tour of the Royal Watercolour Society, Sheffield Mappin Art Gallery, Ruskin Gallery, Stoke on Trent City Museum and Art Gallery, May-October 1986, No 8

The scene depicts soldiers marching to battle in the Franco-Prussian war. In the absence so far of any evidence that he visited the continent in this year, it is difficult to say whether this scene is real or imagined, for it has qualities of immediacy and illustrative strength. In style it is a mixture of 70's restraint and the later confident brightening and loosening of the watercolour evident in the foliage of the trees and the sky and foreground.

Despite the ambiguity given to "Glory", the picture is still tinged with militaristic jingoism and it is interesting to compare this with the uncertain apocalyptic vision of *Portsmouth* (1896).

Portsmouth (1896)

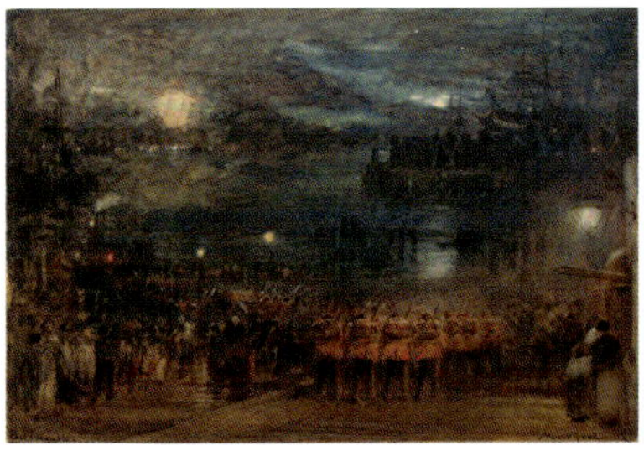

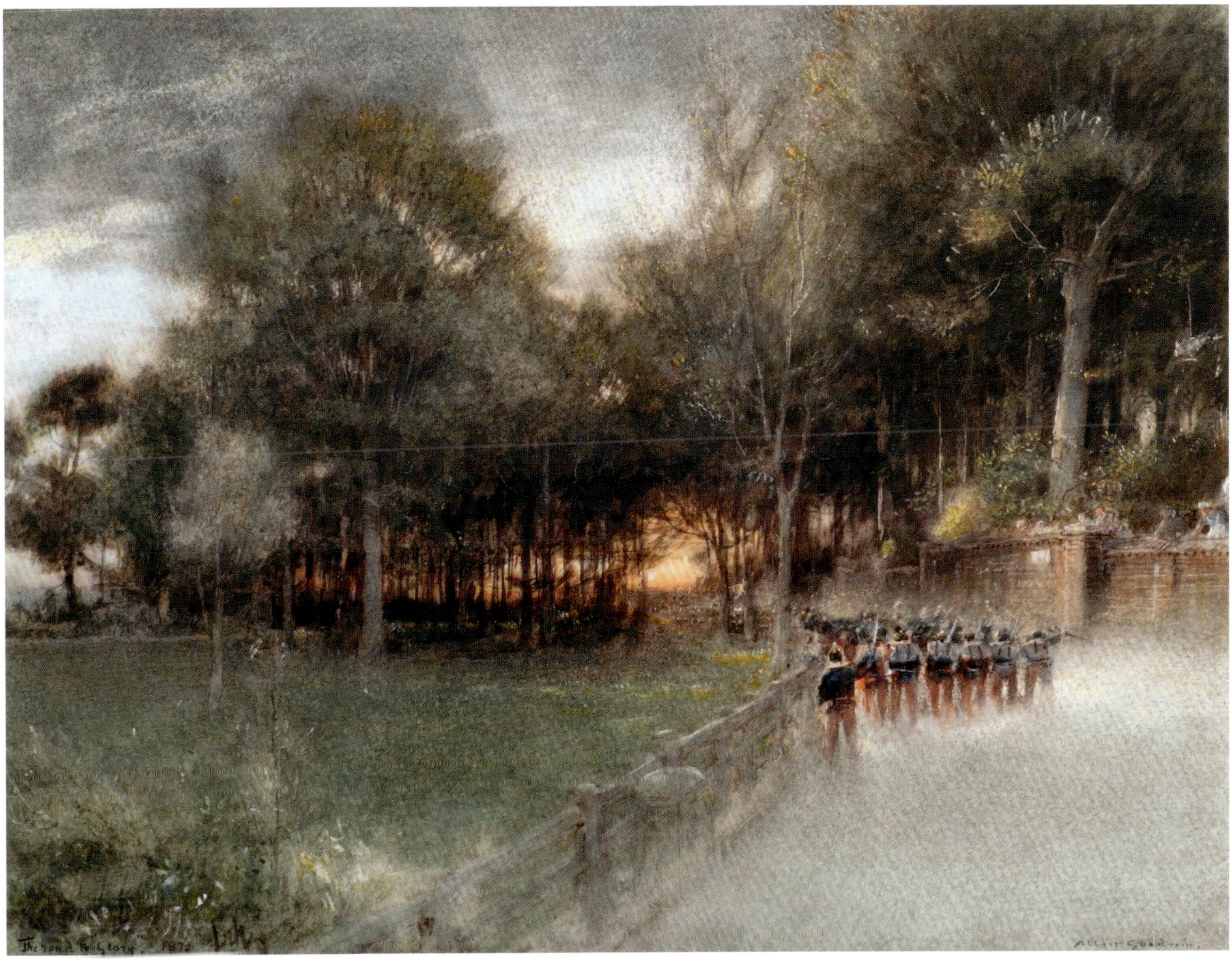

'Also I have a great many questions to ask you, and arrangements to consult you about: and I will give you what price you think right for your drawings as fast as you can make them, and you will get used to me a little before we start for Verona...'

(Letter, Ruskin to Goodwin, Abingdon, 19 March 1871)

'We stopped some time at Assisi; and I liked it better than any of the other places... Goodwin did some beautiful pencil sketches here and the Professor gave him the very highest praise.'
(Arthur Severn, manuscript, John Rylands Library, University of Manchester)

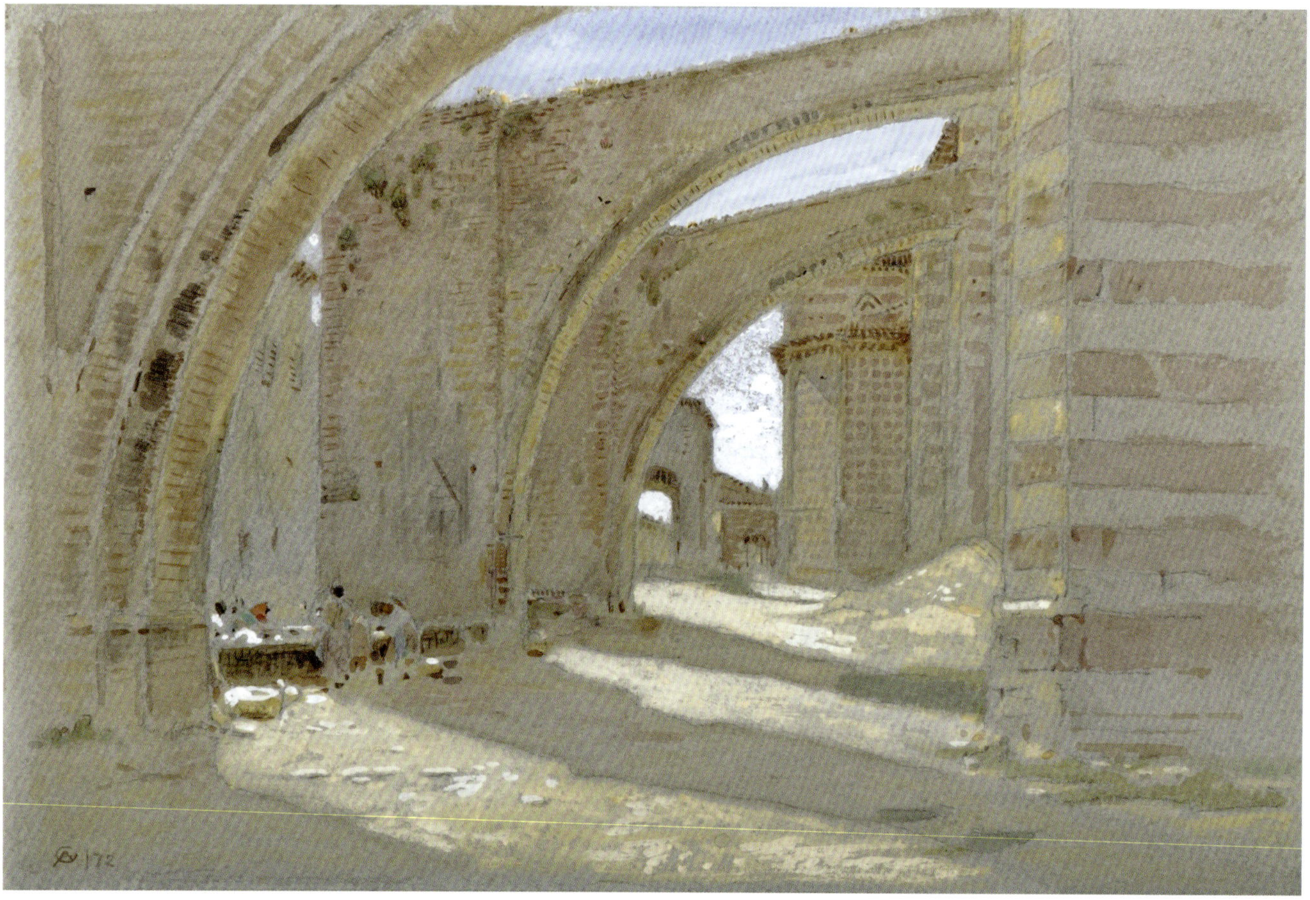

3 **Flying Buttresses at Asissi**
Signed with monogram and dated /72
Watercolour with bodycolour and pencil on tinted paper
5 ¾ x 8 ¼ inches
Exhibited:
Probably the work exhibited at the Society of Painters in Water-Colours, 1873, No 332

In 1872 Albert Goodwin, together with John Ruskin and Arthur Severn amongst others embarked on a sketching tour of Europe. Travelling to Italy via Switzerland and France, they left Rome for their sojourn in Assisi (21-24 May). Ruskin was particularly struck by the majestic flying buttresses at the monastery at Assisi, remarking to Goodwin that they were 'the Fathers of all the flying buttresses'.

'I owe much thanks to Ruskin, who ballyragged me into love of form when I was getting too content with colour alone: and colour alone is luxury.

Remembering how much I enjoyed the three months I had when I took up with drawing when with Ruskin in Italy; and how good it was for one. The pleasure that is to be found in lines *which should string a drawing together is almost an unknown quantity in these days of paint and paint only.'*

(*The Diary of Albert Goodwin, RWS, 1883-1927*, Privately Printed, 1934, Page 37, 18 July 1900 and Page 183, 1 June 1913)

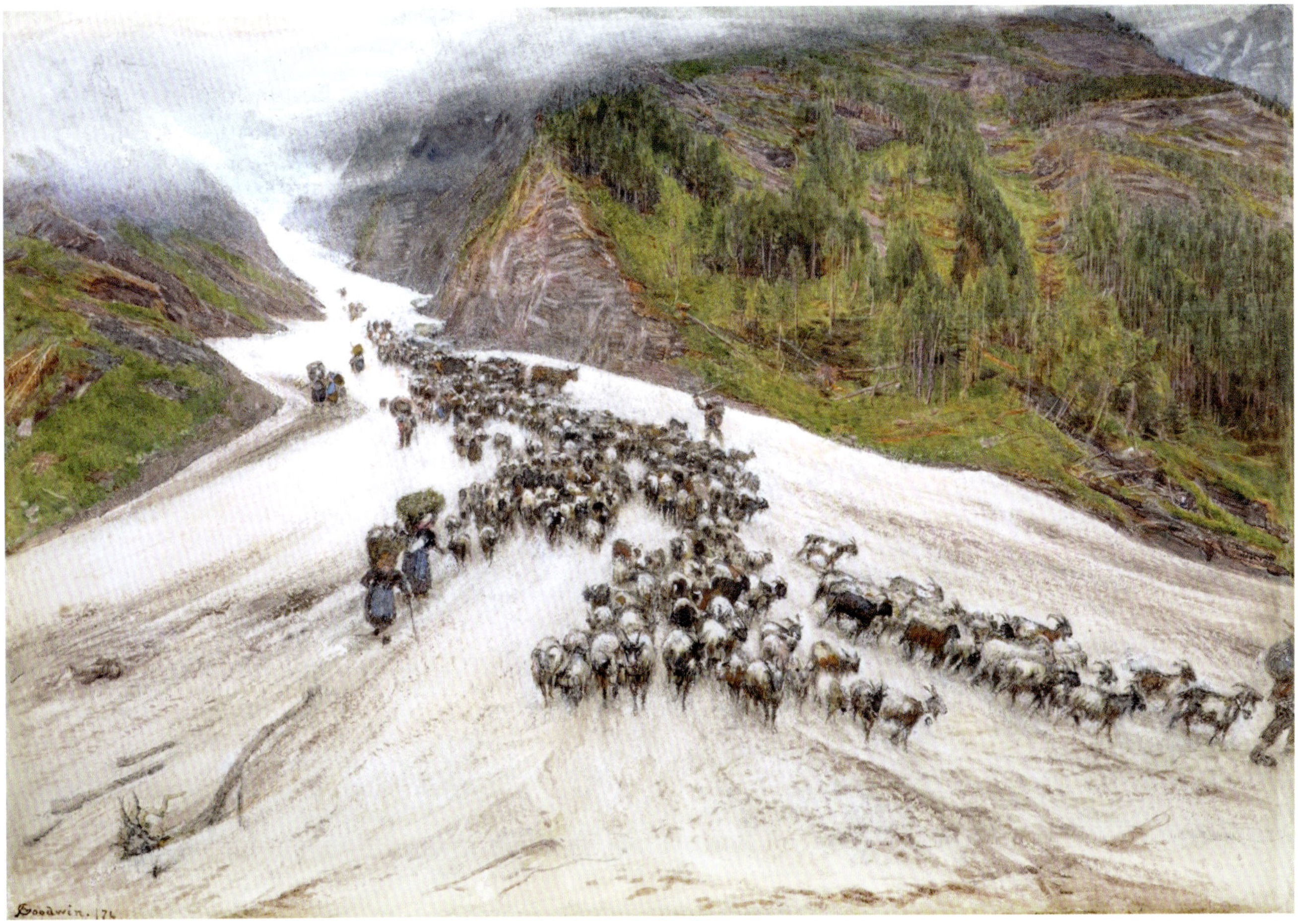

4 **The Goat-Herd in the Swiss Alps**
Signed and dated /74
Watercolour
10 x 14 ¼ inches
Literature:
Albert Goodwin RWS, 1845-1932, London: Chris Beetles Ltd, 1986, Limited Edition of 1000, Plate 15
Exhibited:
Albert Goodwin RWS 1845-1932. 129 of His Best Works Borrowed From Private Collections.
A Museum Tour of the Royal Watercolour Society, Sheffield Mappin Art Gallery, Ruskin Gallery, Stoke on Trent City Museum and Art Gallery, May-October 1986, No 17

'Thank God for a safe return. We found a letter saying that Mother would be at Salisbury, and our ship getting in at 6 a.m. we came on, reaching here at 10 a.m. Olive's squeal of delight when she saw our faces at the carriage window was our first welcome, though the lovely landscape had smiled a welcome to us long before. Now we are at last with those we love, and I suppose the whole past three months will soon be as a dream.

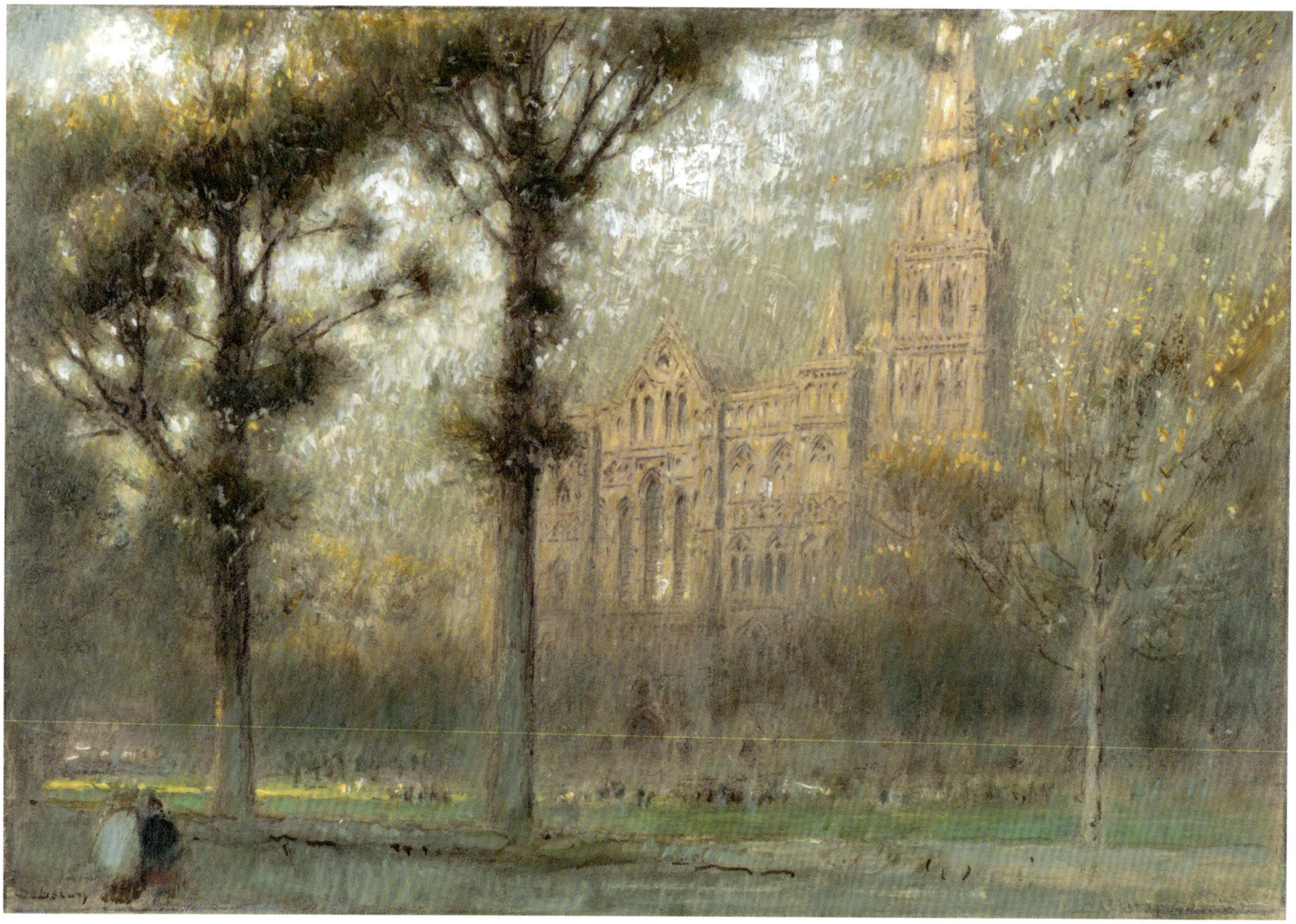

5 **Salisbury**
Signed and inscribed with title
Oil on tinted paper
10 x 13 ¾ inches

It seemed curious that yesterday I was at sea in my cabin working on the memory of Niagara; this evening out on old Sarum making a sketch of that. How glad am I our travels are over. Have still to get to the others on Saturday and leave here on that day for Ilfracombe. What a new face the English country has for one after America, the delightful sense of venerableness and reverent age in the habitations of men, while Salisbury Close never looked more entrancing.'

(*The Diary of Albert Goodwin, RWS, 1883-1927*, Privately Printed, 1934, Page 84, 8 May 1902)

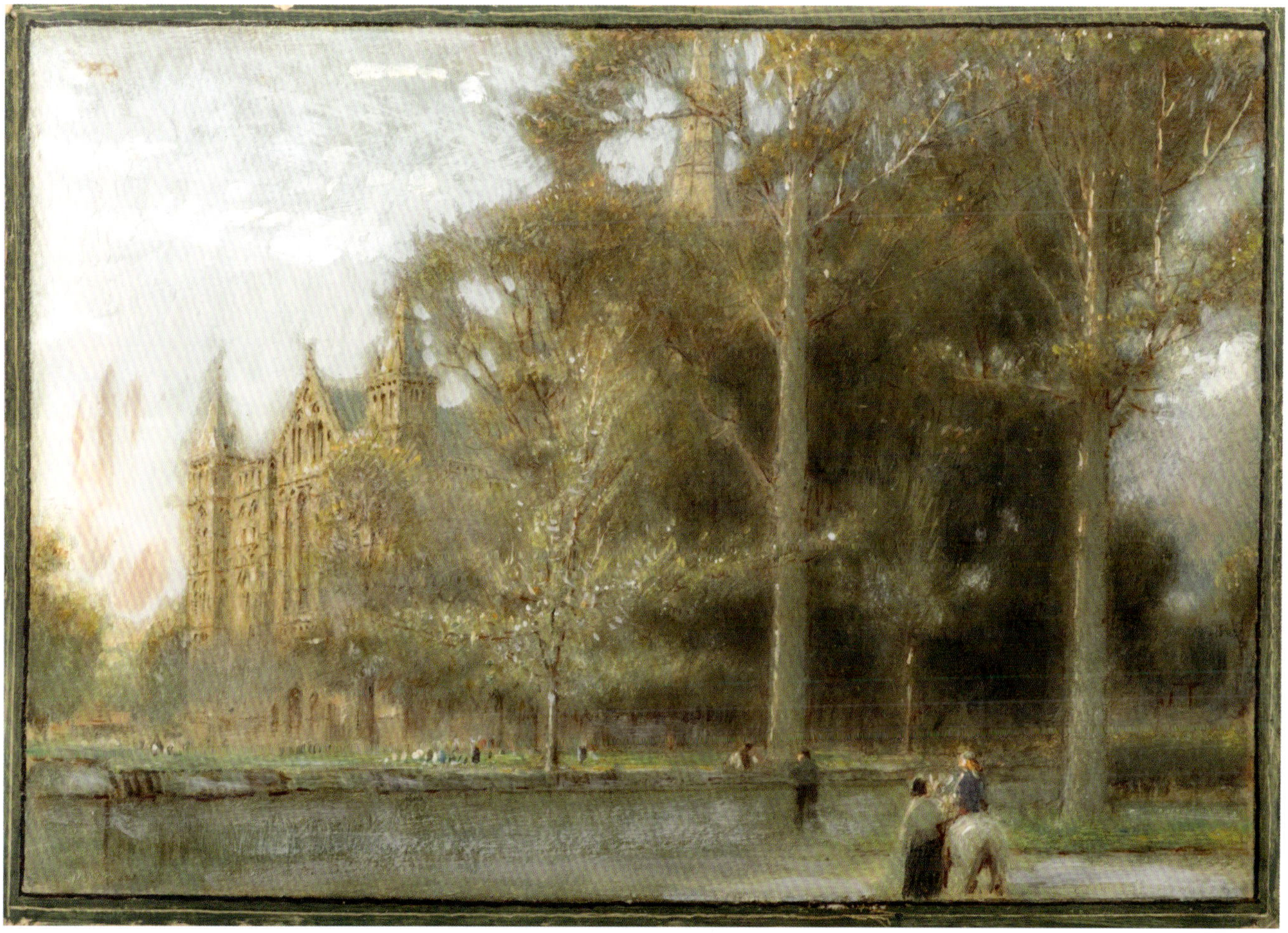

6 **Salisbury Cathedral**
Oil on paper enclosed by a decorative border
10 ½ x 14 ¼ inches

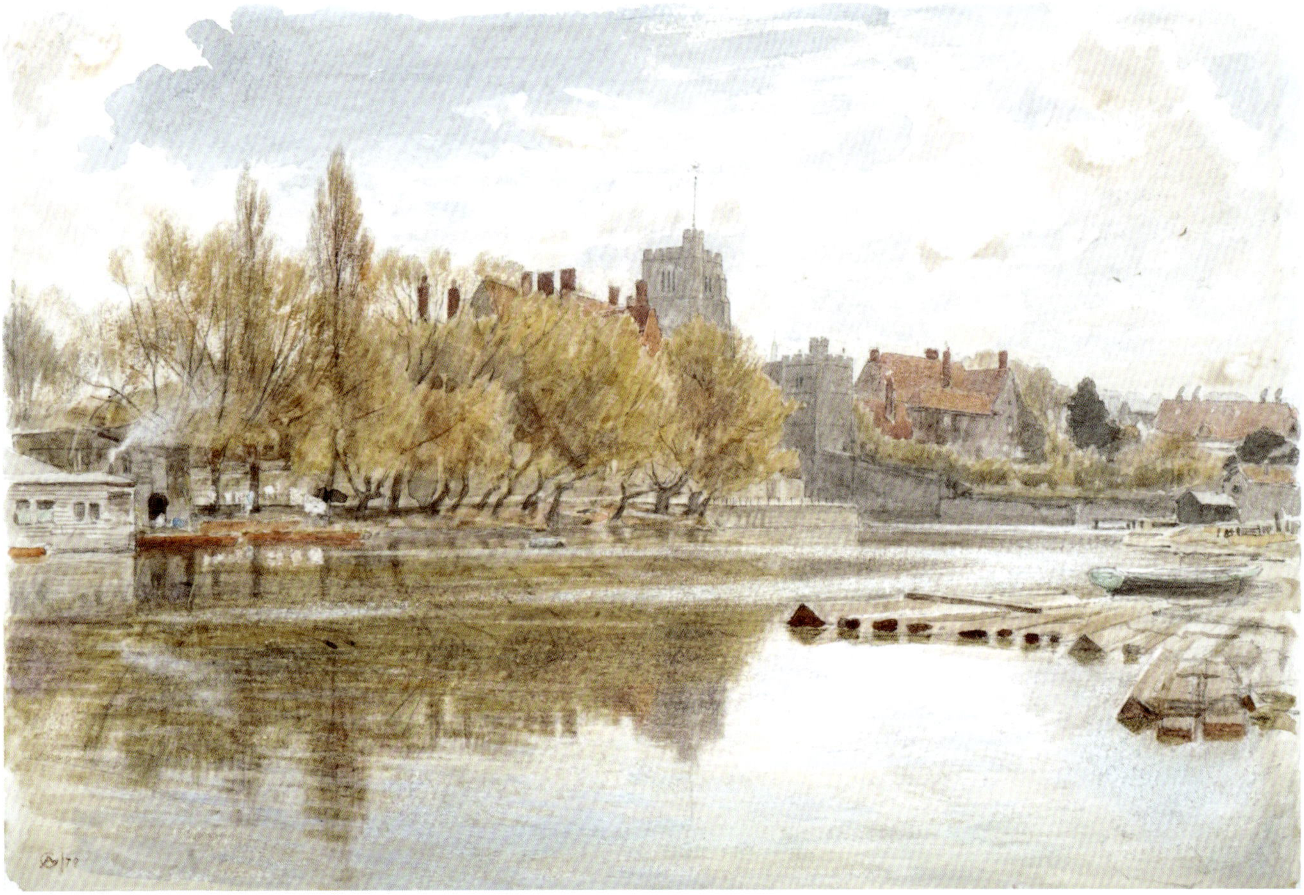

7 Maidstone
Signed with monogram and dated /79
Watercolour
7 x 10 inches
Literature:
Hammond Smith, *Albert Goodwin RWS*, Leigh-on-Sea: F Lewis, 1977, Plate 16

Albert Goodwin remained attached to his birthplace of Maidstone in Kent, and often returned there both to visit his family and to paint. He was inevitably drawn to the impressive panorama that is laid out along the north bank of the River Medway and centres on the historic Archbishop's Palace (dating to the fourteenth and sixteenth centuries) and All Saints Church (built in the late fourteenth century as part of the College of All Saints newly founded by Archbishop Courtenay). In 1885, Goodwin's brother, Harry, would paint a more distant view, which shows that the land south of the river remained as fields.

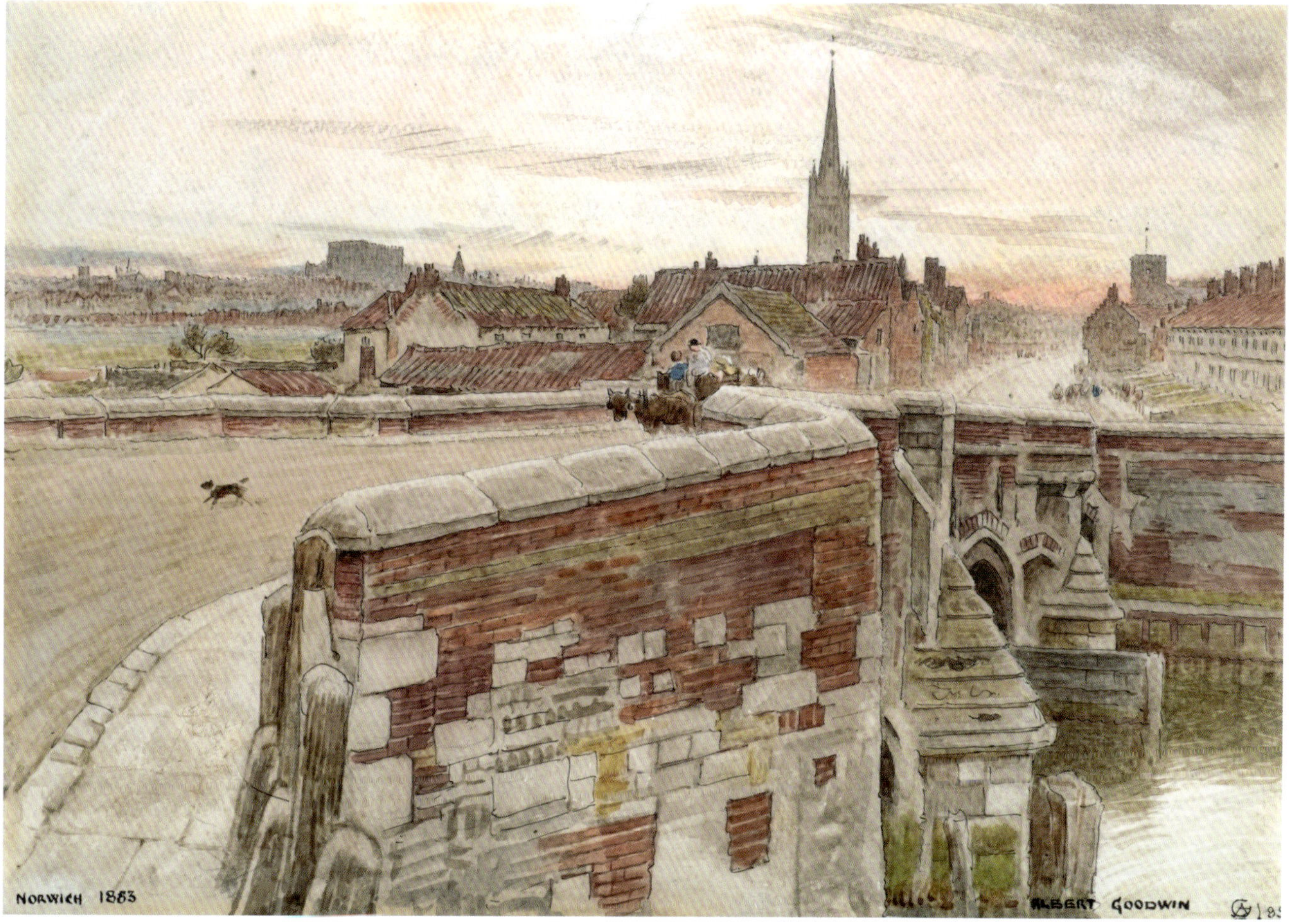

8 Norwich
Signed with monogram and dated /85
Inscribed 'Albert Goodwin Norwich 1863' in another hand
Watercolour with pen and ink
7 x 9 ¾ inches

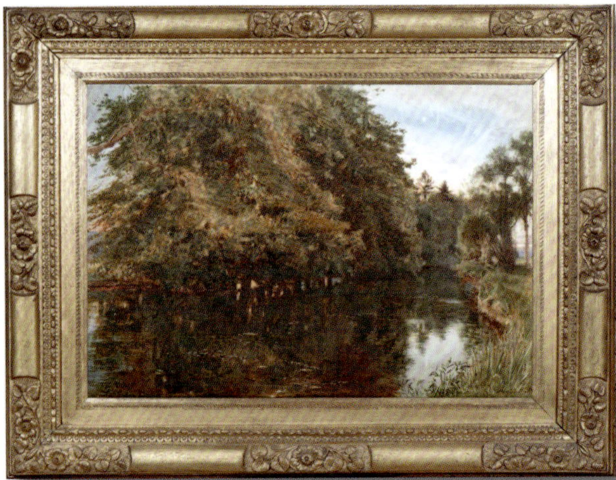

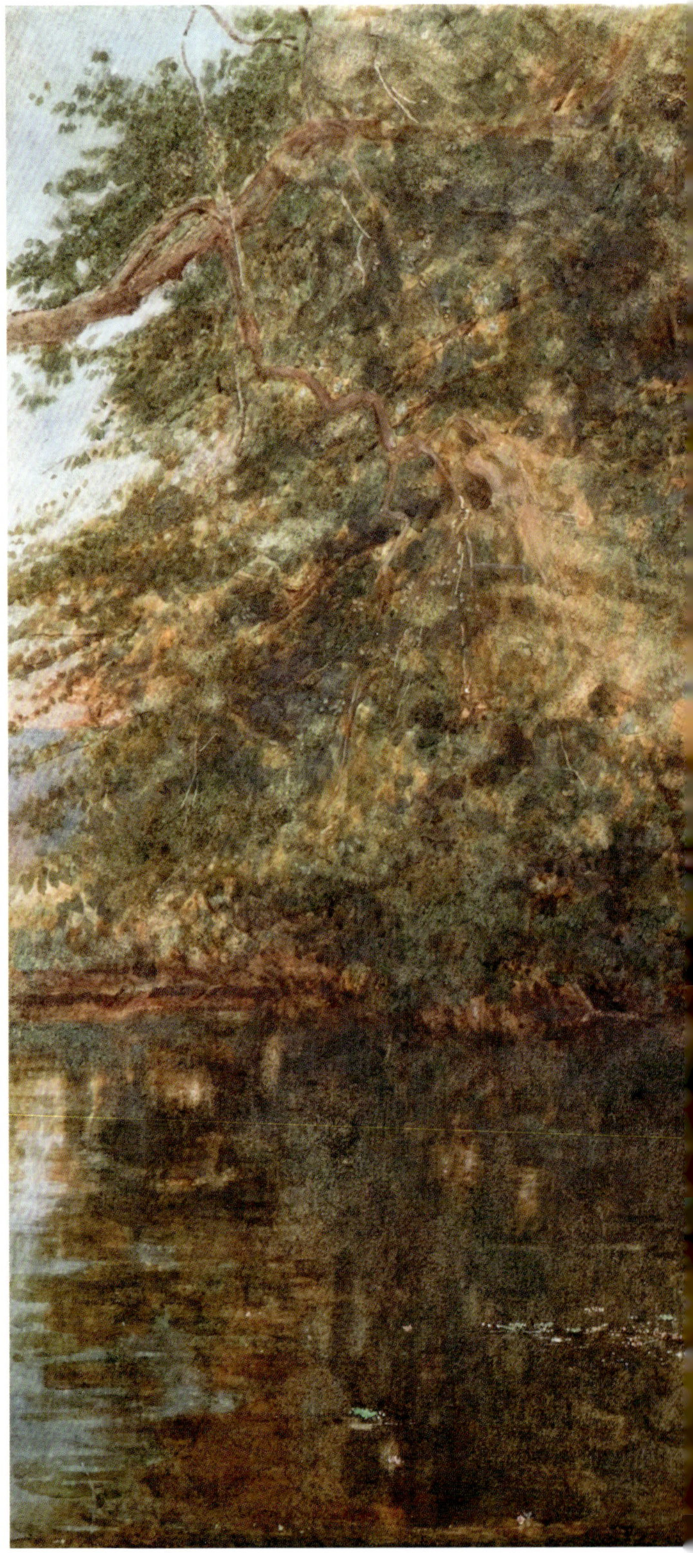

9 **Silence, "Here with fantastic garlands came Ophelia"**
Signed and dated 1884
Inscribed with title on a label on reverse and further inscribed '3. Silence £100. "Here with fantastic garlands came Ophelia" see "Hamlet"
Watercolour with bodycolour
22 x 30 ½ inches
Exhibited:
Royal Society of Painters in Water-Colours, Summer 1884, No 7; The Graves Art Gallery, Birmingham, as "Here with fantastic garlands came Ophelia" and "A Thames backwater"

In original carved, gilded oak frame by Charles Goodwin.

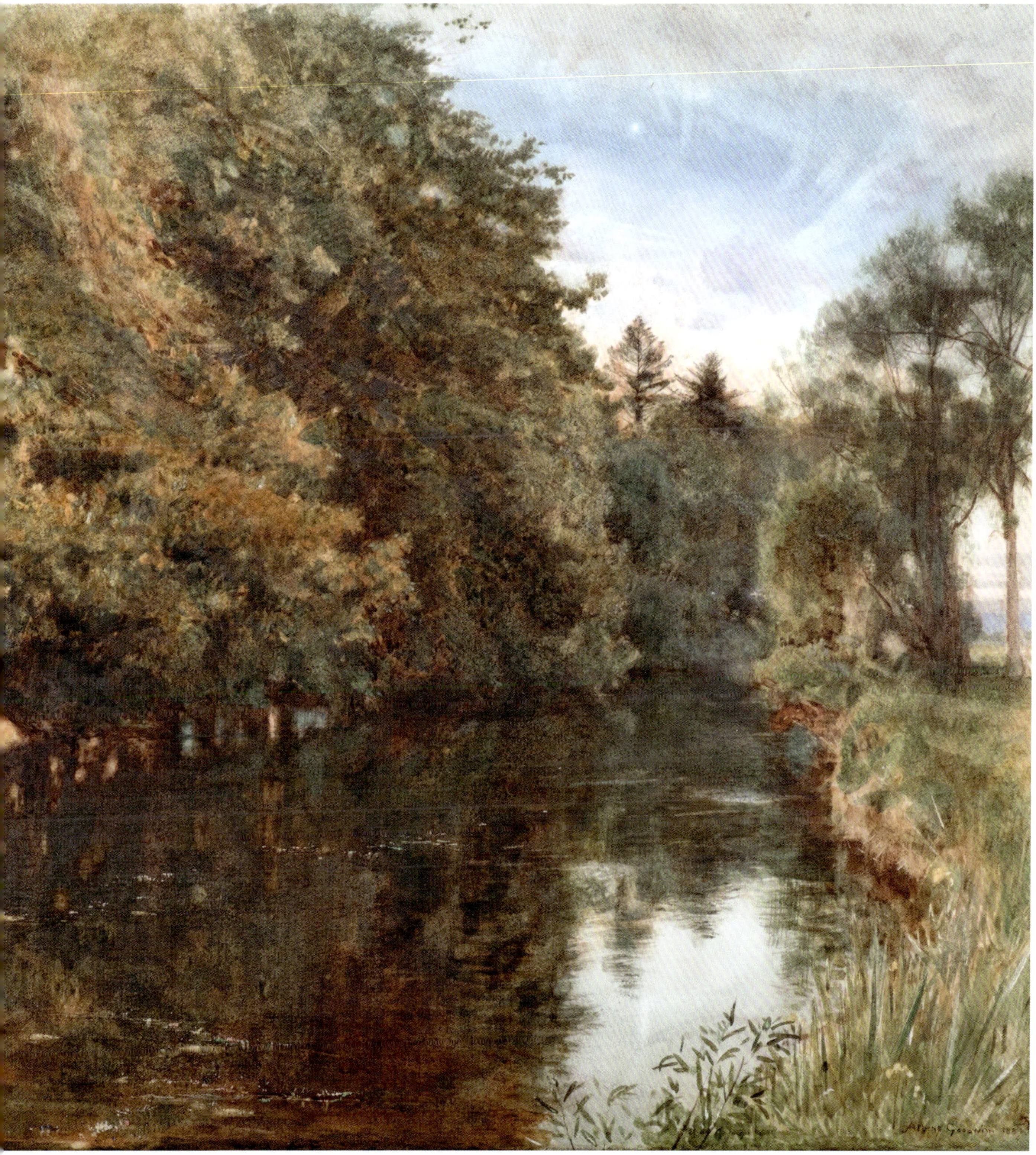

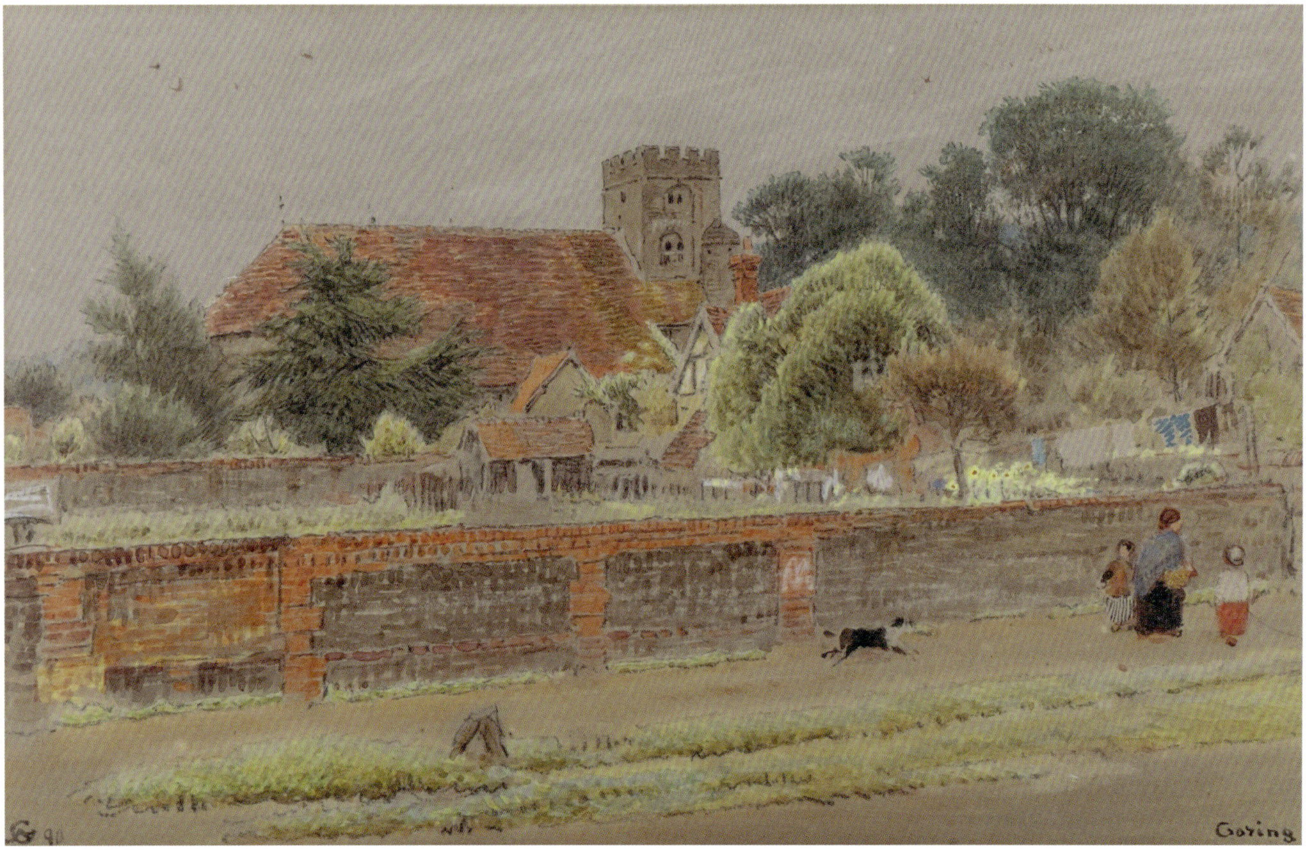

10 **Goring**
Signed with monogram, inscribed with title and dated 90
Watercolour with bodycolour on tinted paper
6 ½ x 9 ½ inches
Exhibited:
Probably the work exhibited at 'A Collection of Water-Colour Drawings of Many-Sided Nature By Albert Goodwin, RWS', Fine Art Society, London, May 1890, no 68 as 'Goring on Thames';
The Fine Art Society, London, May 1968

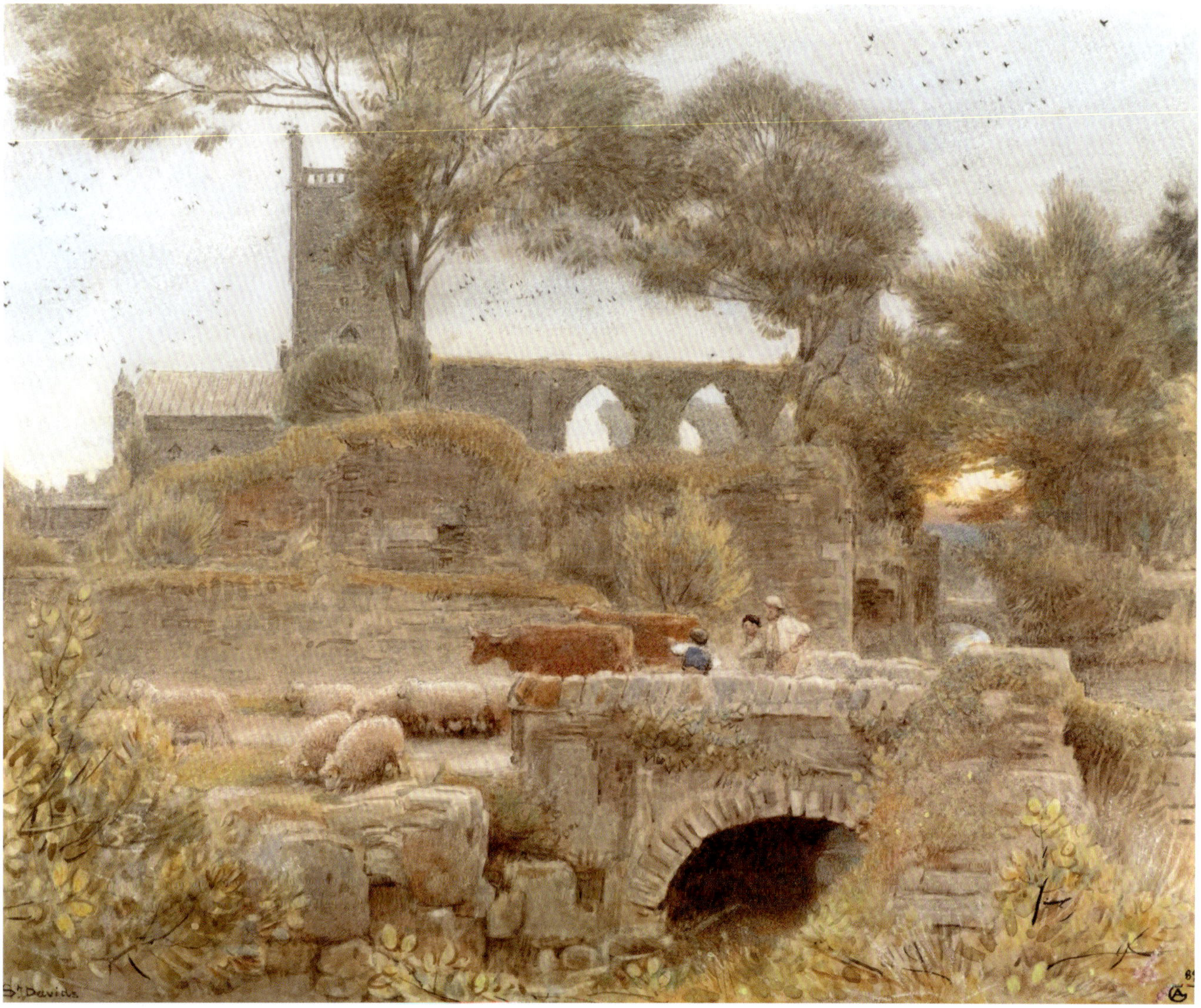

11 St Davids
Signed with monogram, inscribed with title and dated 89
Watercolour
8 ½ x 10 inches
Literature:
Albert Goodwin RWS, 1845-1932, London: Chris Beetles Ltd, 1986, Limited Edition of 1000, Plate 38
Exhibited:
Royal Society of Painters in Water-Colours, Winter 1889, no 343

The ruins of St Davids Bishops Palace, Pembrokeshire, are sited on the opposite bank of the river Alun (seen in the foreground) to St Davids Cathedral. The original monastery was established by St David in the 6th century and for the next 400 years was subjected to regular attacks by Norse raiders. In the 11th century the Normans undertook extensive ecclesiastical building work including many defensive walls. Successive bishops added to the Palace and the ruins depicted are largely from the late 13th and 14th centuries.

'If there is an undue proportion of sketches of Whitby, its exceeding picturequeness must plead for it; as far as I have seen there is no town in England like unto it in its wealth of colour. Durham is nobler in many ways, but a change one regrets is slowly coming over all these ruddy North of England towns. Whenever a tiled roof falls in or gets worn out, it is replaced by slate, the result being cold grey instead of a pleasant, warm, Venetian red. Albert Goodwin.'

(From a note to "A collection of drawings in City, Town and Hamlet" Fine Art Society, May 1886)

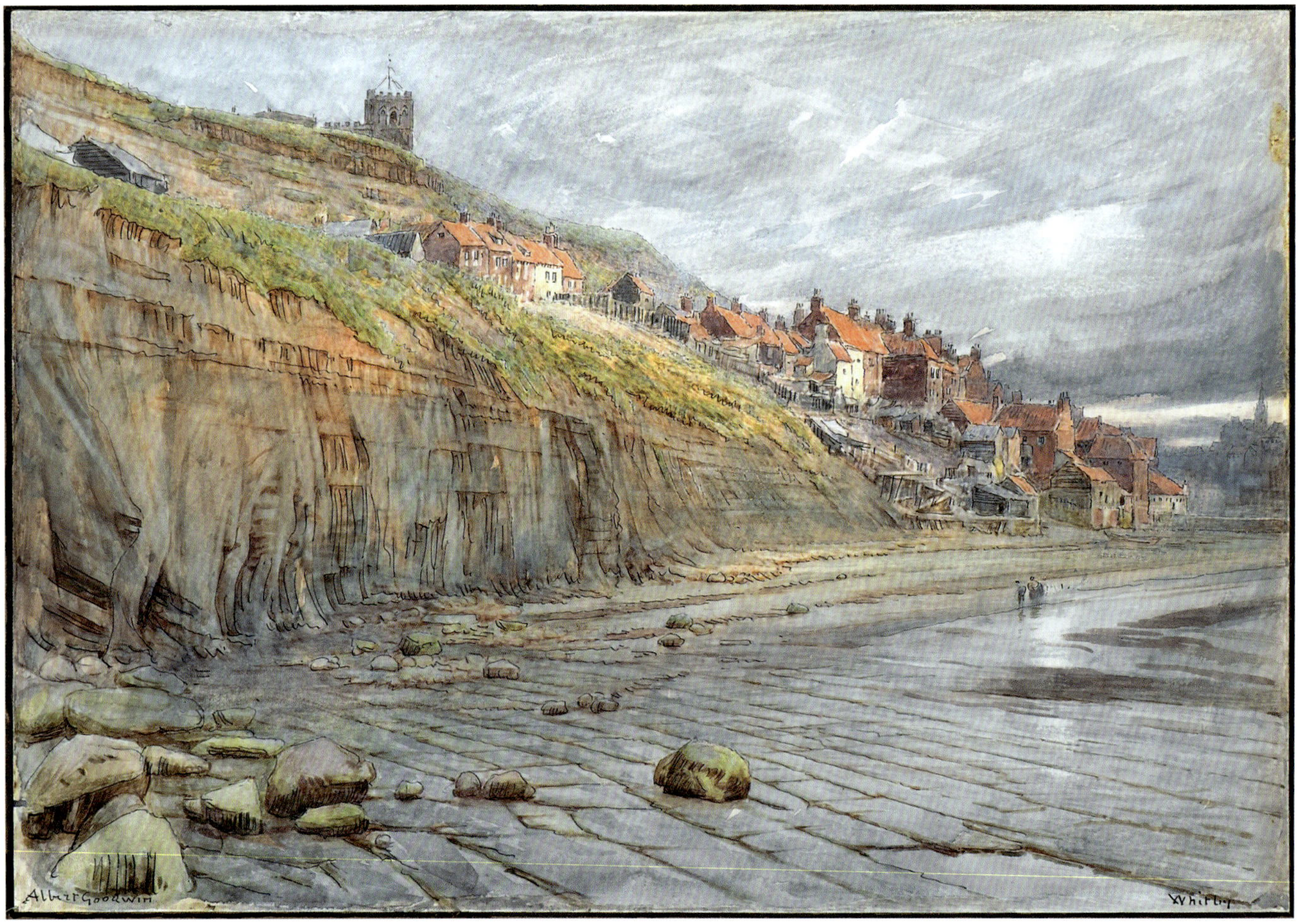

12 **Whitby**
Signed and inscribed with title
Watercolour with pen and ink
10 ¼ x 14 ¼ inches
Literature:
Hammond Smith, *Albert Goodwin RWS*, Leigh-on-Sea: F Lewis, 1977, Plate 37;
Albert Goodwin RWS, 1845-1932, London: Chris Beetles Ltd, 1986, Limited Edition of 1000, Plate 30

From a diary entry we know that Albert Goodwin visited Whitby in March 1891, and in May wrote
'The transforming power of the sunlight, how it glorifies and elevates the most common objects, even having no beauty of their own, are invested with it under the sunshine!'

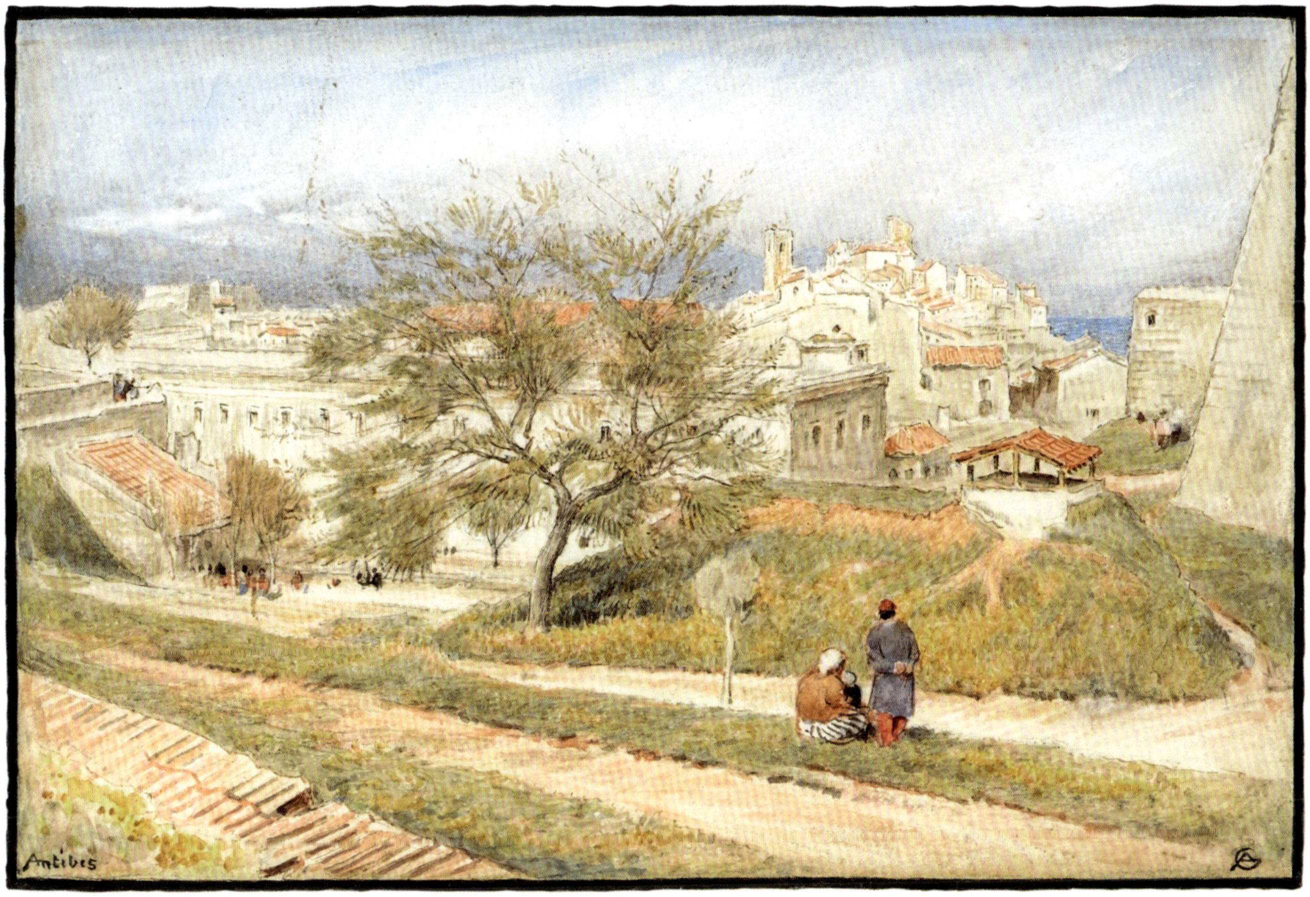

13 Antibes, Cote D'Azur, France

Signed with monogram and inscribed 'Antibes'

Watercolour

6 ¼ x 9 ¼ inches

Literature:

Hammond Smith, *Albert Goodwin RWS*, Leigh-on-Sea: F Lewis, 1977, Plate 14

Exhibited:

Probably the painting exhibited at the Royal Society of Painters in Water-Colours, Winter 1891, no 59

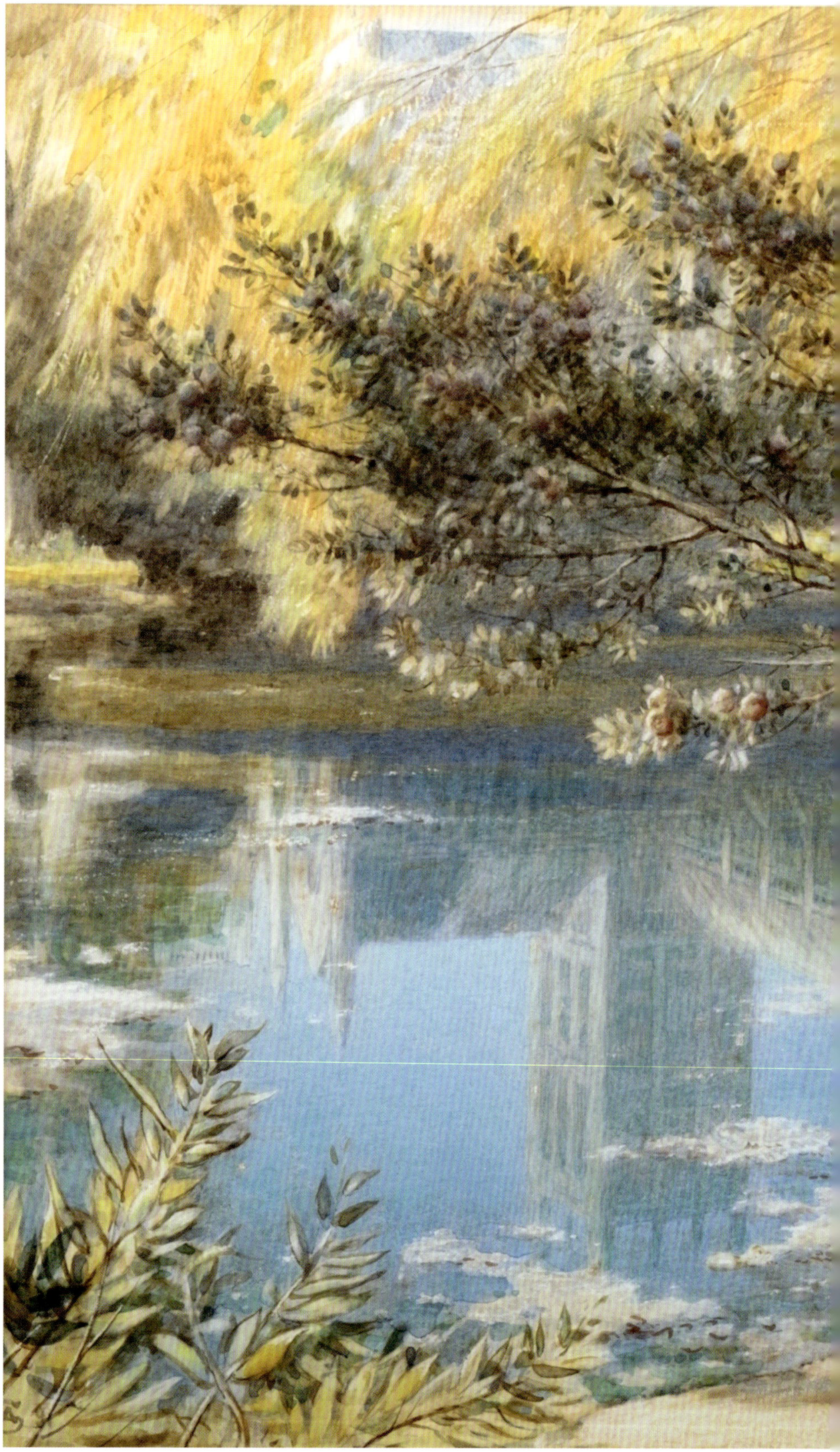

14 Wells
Signed with monogram and dated /91
Watercolour
14 x 20 ½ inches
Exhibited:
'Chris Beetles Summer Show',
Chris Beetles Gallery, London, 2003, No 14

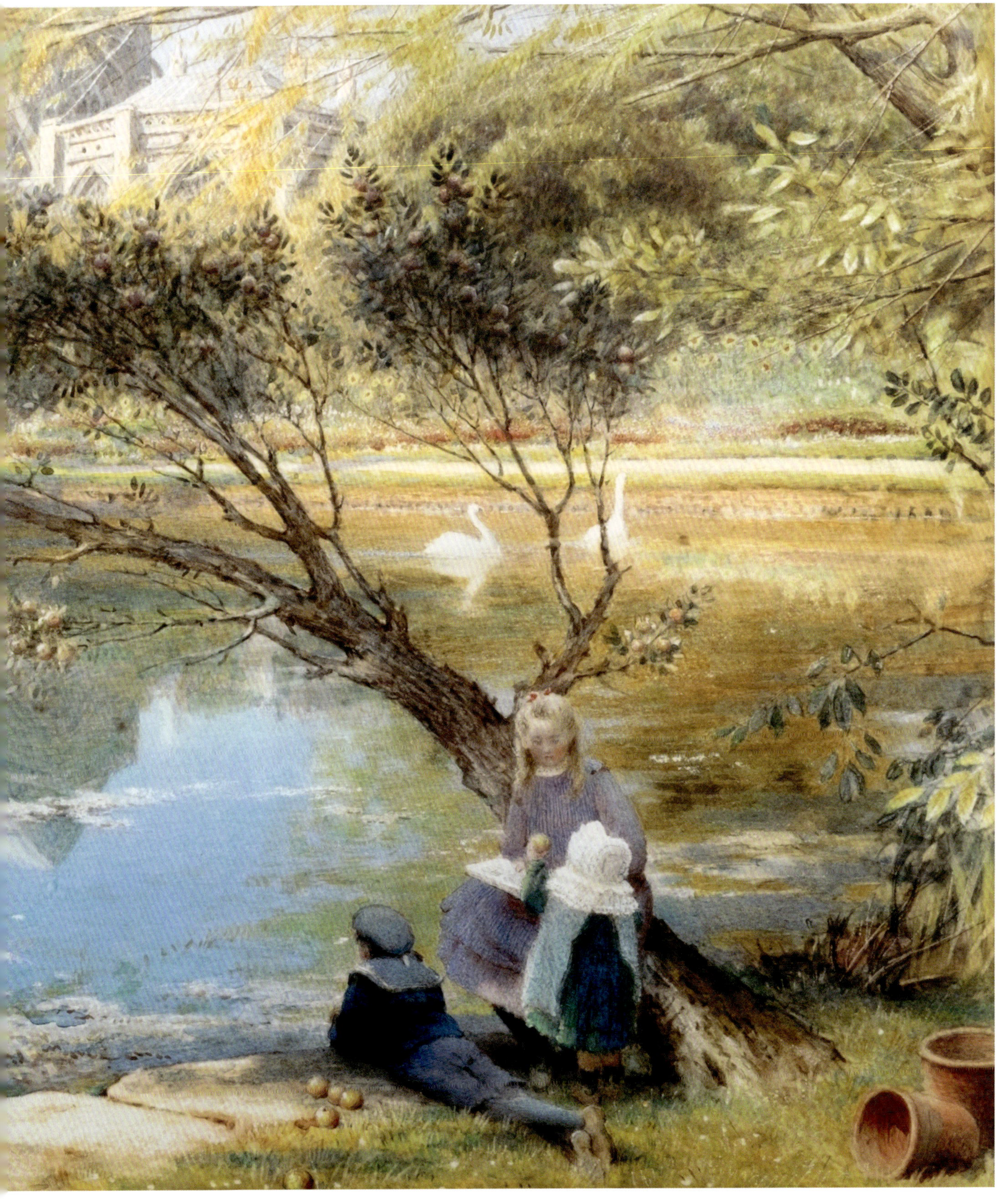

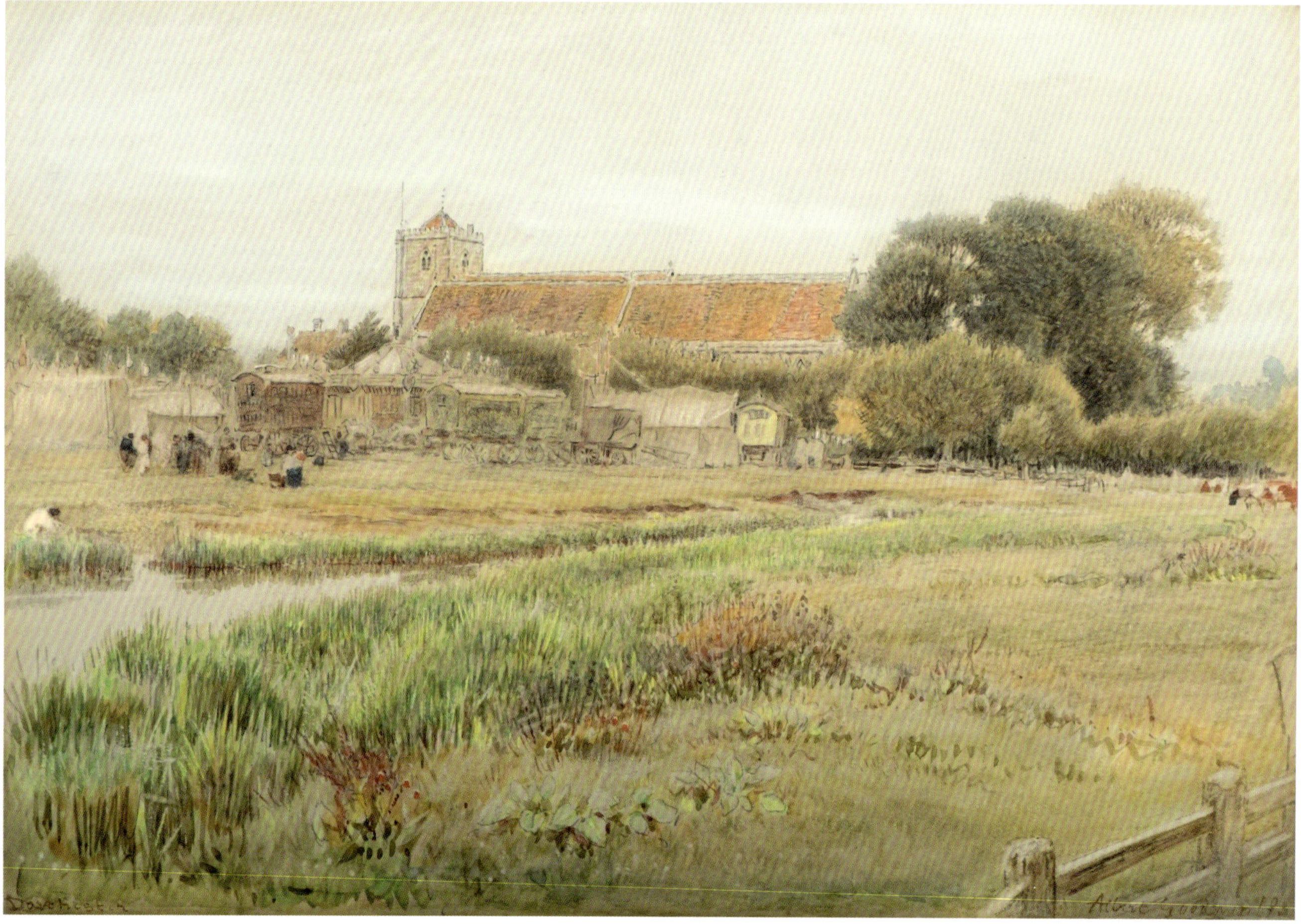

15 **Dorchester**
Signed, inscribed with title and dated /93
Watercolour
9 ½ x 13 ½ inches

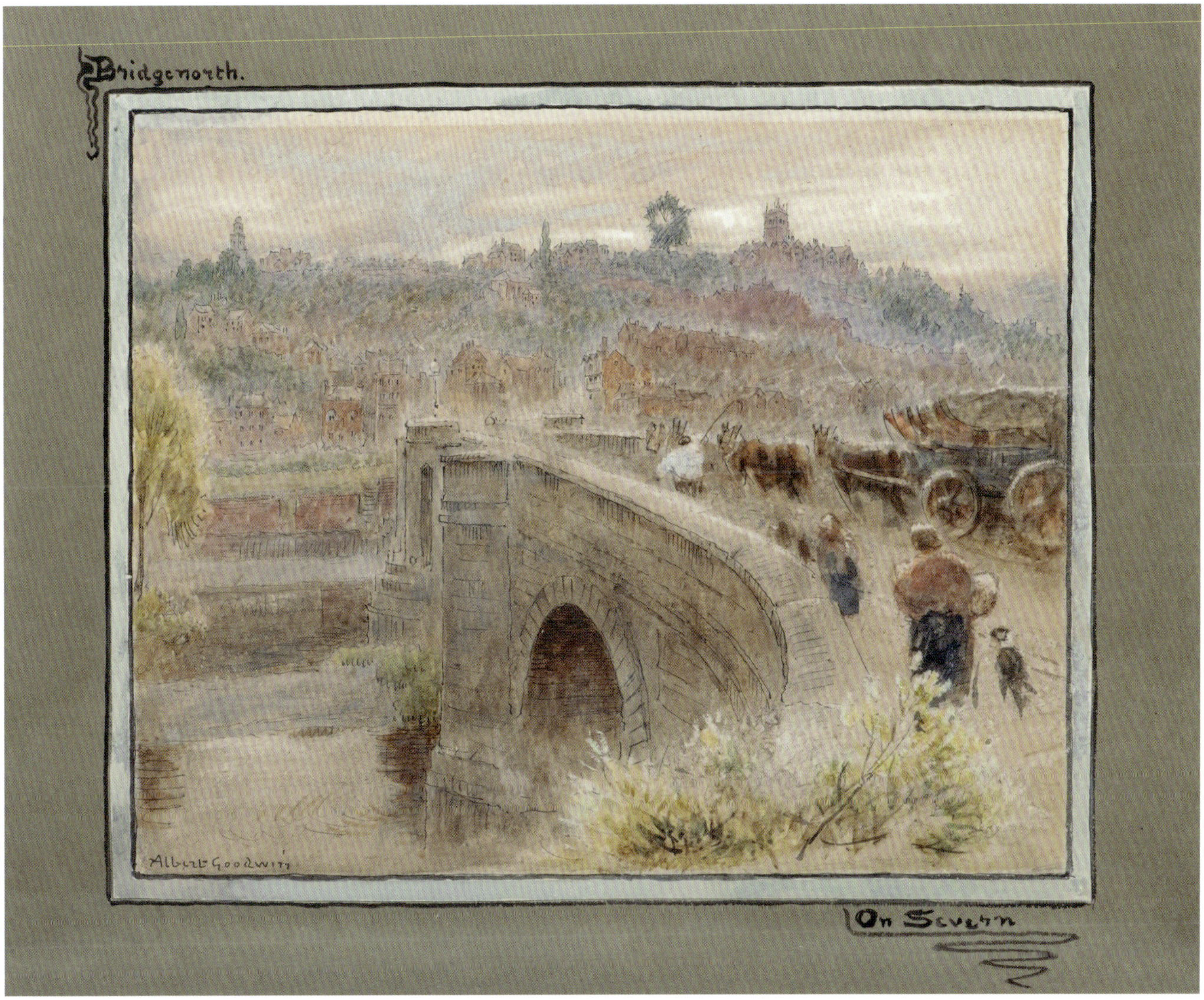

16 Bridgenorth On Severn
Signed and inscribed with title
Watercolour enclosed by a decorative border
9 ½ x 10 ¼ inches

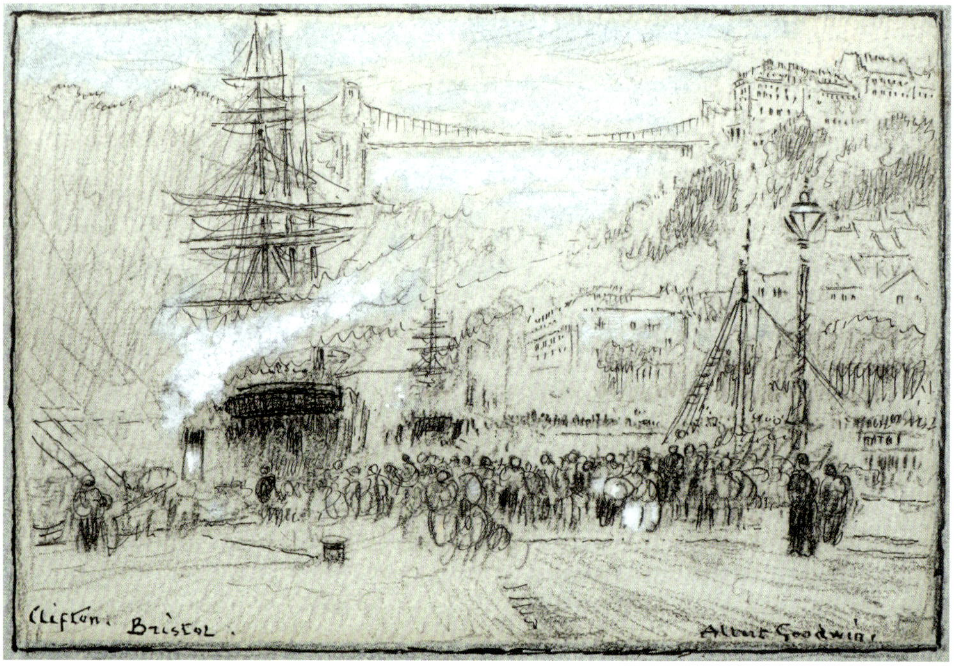

17 **Clifton, Bristol** (left)
Signed and inscribed with title
Ink, chalk and bodycolour
6 x 8 ¾ inches

18 **Canterbury** (below)
Signed and inscribed with title
Black and white chalk
10 x 13 ¾ inches

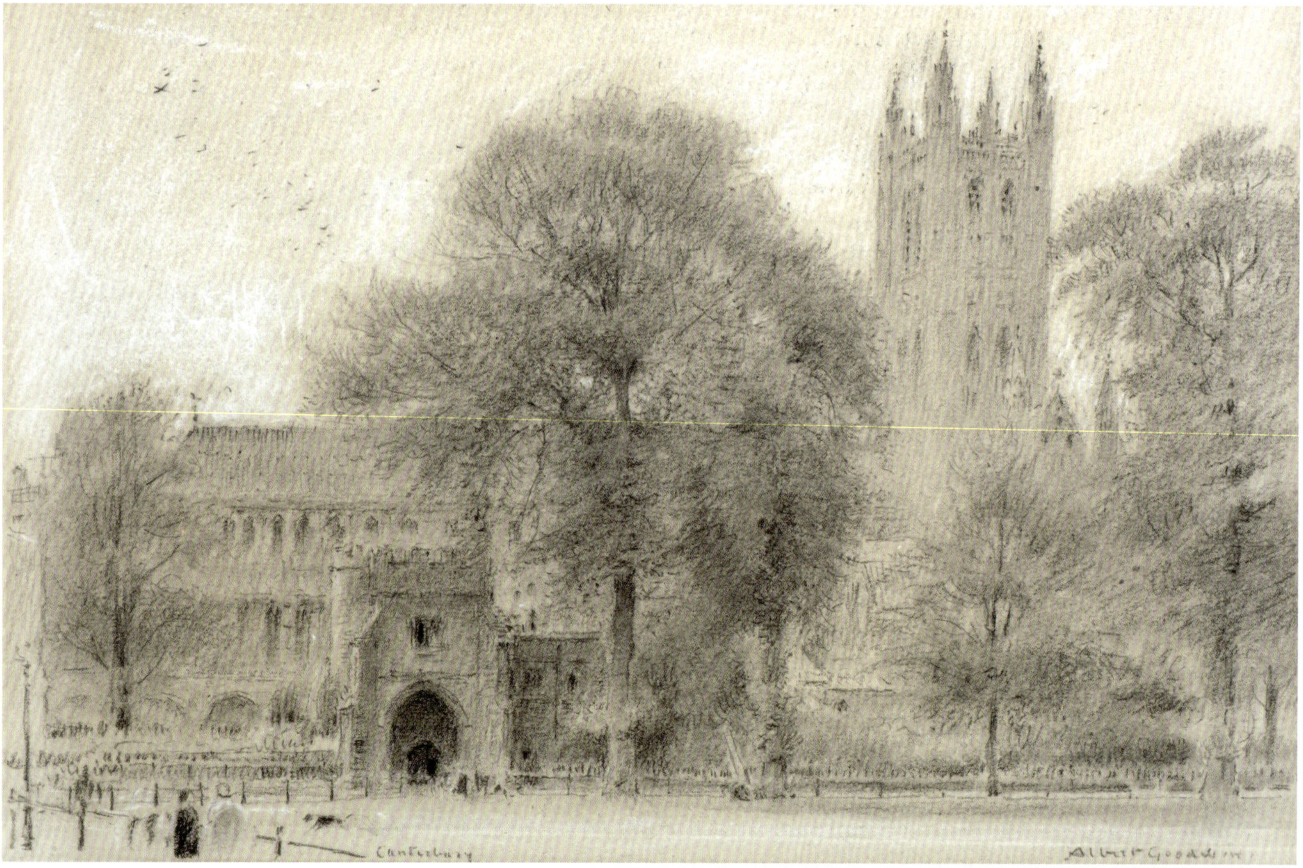

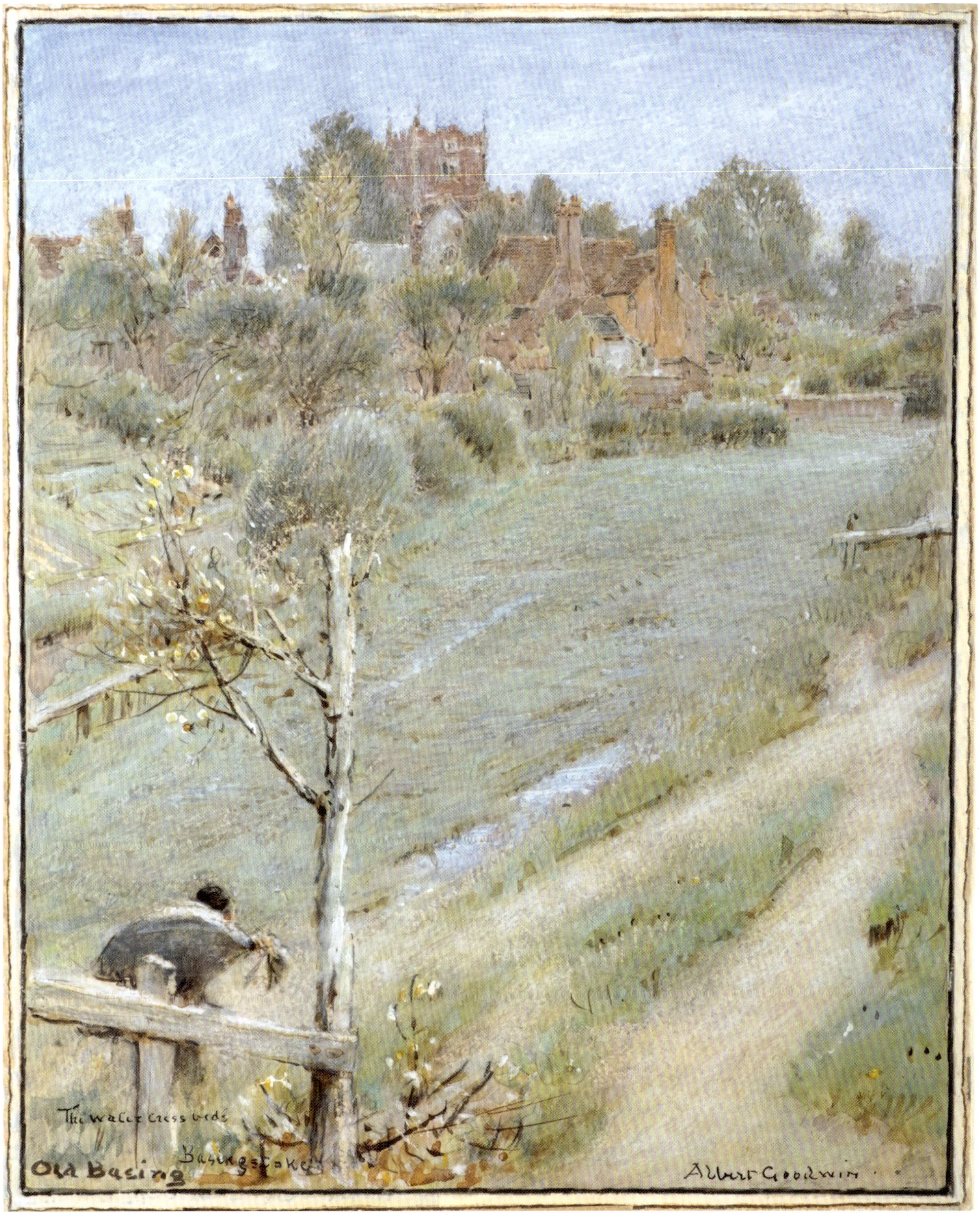

19 **Old Basing.**
The Watercress Beds, Basingstoke
Signed and inscribed with title
Watercolour and bodycolour enclosed by a decorative border
10 ½ x 8 ¼ inches

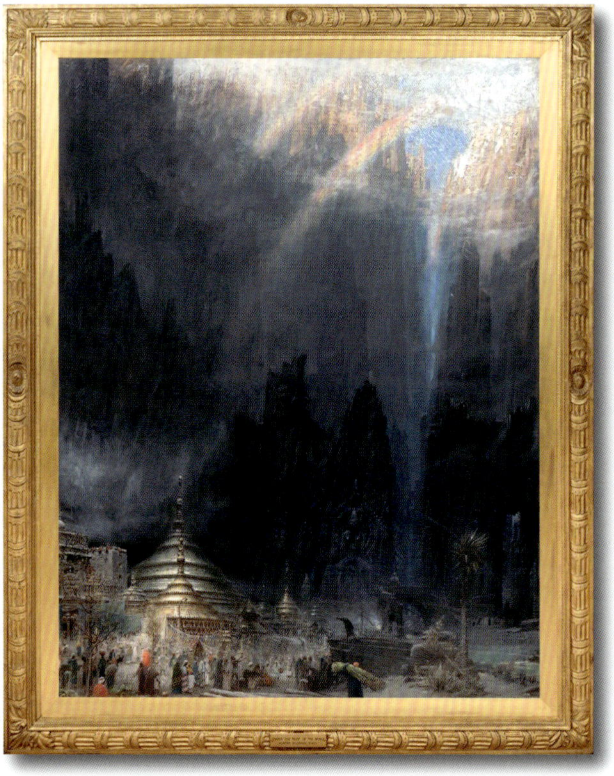

'I intend this to epitomise my impression of India where beauty and horror seem always to "jostle" each other. A missionary is seen preaching the Gospel. Near him the while, hook-swinging and other frightfulness is in progress, and his preaching is derided. "Alexander the Coppersmith" holds up his idols in opposition, while the people look on with indifference. Parabolically there is a way "up and out" if the people will only see it and use it, up and out to a better country'

(Albert Goodwin's note accompanying the City of Birmingham exhibition, 1926)

20 **Under the Roof of the World**
Signed and dated 1897
Oil on canvas
56 x 41 ¼ inches
Exhibited:
Royal Academy of Arts, 1898, No 298;
'A collection of oil paintings, water colour drawings etc
By Albert Goodwin, RWS, RWA Lent by M B Walker Esq',
City of Birmingham Museum and Art Gallery, 1926, no 136

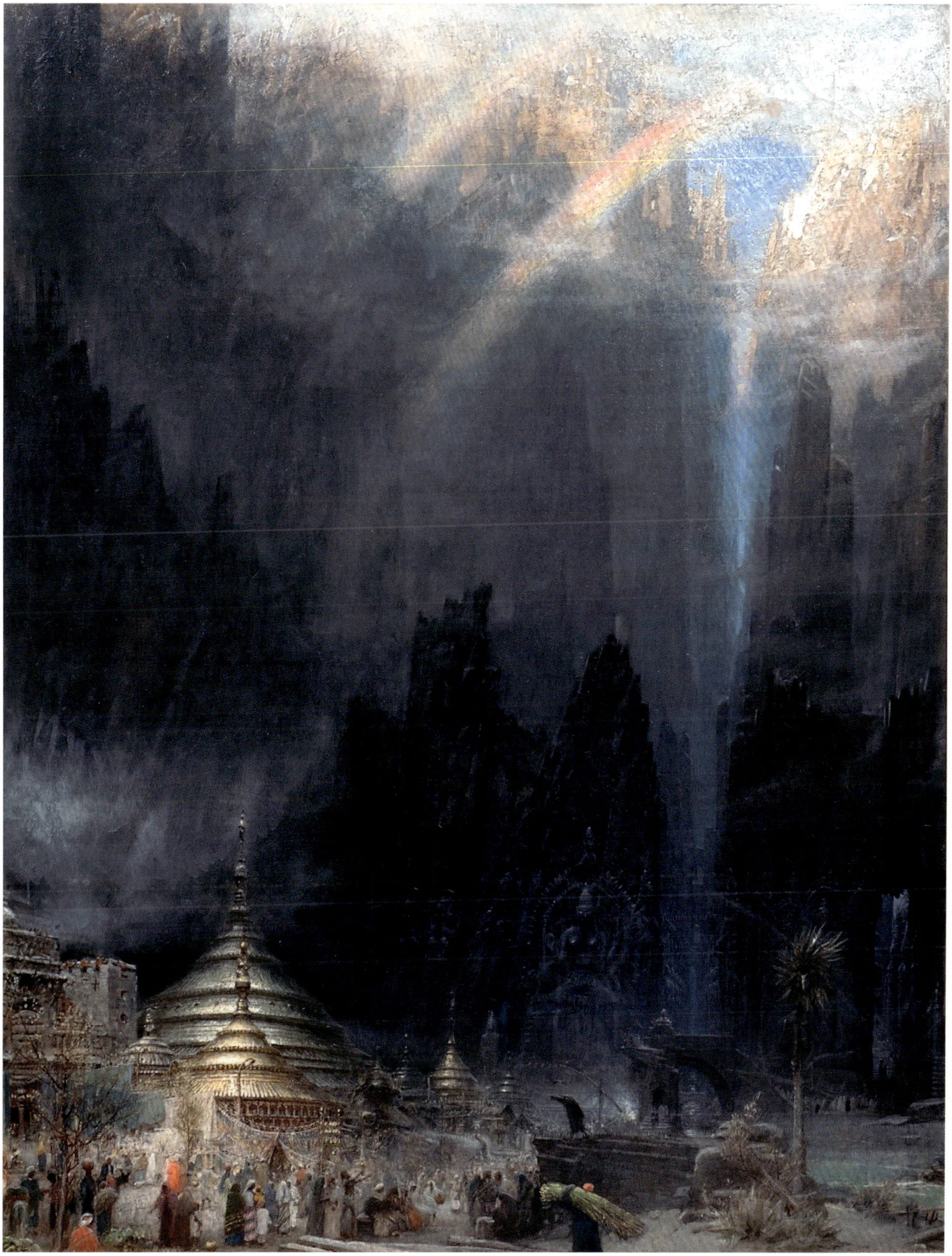

'Reached Port Said yesterday morning, and after waiting half the morning in cold wet draught of wind, got to Cairo at 5 p.m. Too late to go round and look for lodgings, so spent the night at the Bristol Hotel; mistaking it for Hotel de Nil, where I stayed when with the wife and Ivy and "Sairey" some thirty-two years ago!'

(*The Diary of Albert Goodwin, RWS, 1883-1927*, Privately Printed, 1934, Page 90, 22 January 1909)

'Removed from Suisse Pension, which was Suisse in nothing save the name! food, too awful. Have now a cheerful south bedroom in apartments kept by a Mrs Scott. A lady reminding me in many ways of David Copperfield's aunt, and quite capable of tackling triumphantly as many Miss Murdstones as care to "come on!" Shall have been in this cheerful room a week to-morrow; a week that has been, if with ups and downs, yet I have done, and enjoyed doing, some drawing out on the Mohattan Hills, an old subject of mine, but one that might well be done again and again. So for these great blessing of renewed health, I ought to be exceeding grateful; expecially to find myself able to work is delightful; for spending money extravagantly with no results would have been to me dreadful. Went one day to the Tombs of the Caliphes, but remembering my former unpleasant experience with the Arabs there, I had a man and a donkey. My donkey man (a silent morose man) took me through the solitary lanes and dead streets, winding about, seemingly quite aimlessly. I was not at all sure of him and I suppose I got reminded of that other experience: so that, when at a particularly dark, silent corner, he suddenly said, "No man die before life finish!" I instantly felt round for a weapon of offence.'

(*The Diary of Albert Goodwin, RWS, 1883-1927*, Privately Printed, 1934, Pages 91 & 92, 30 January 1909)

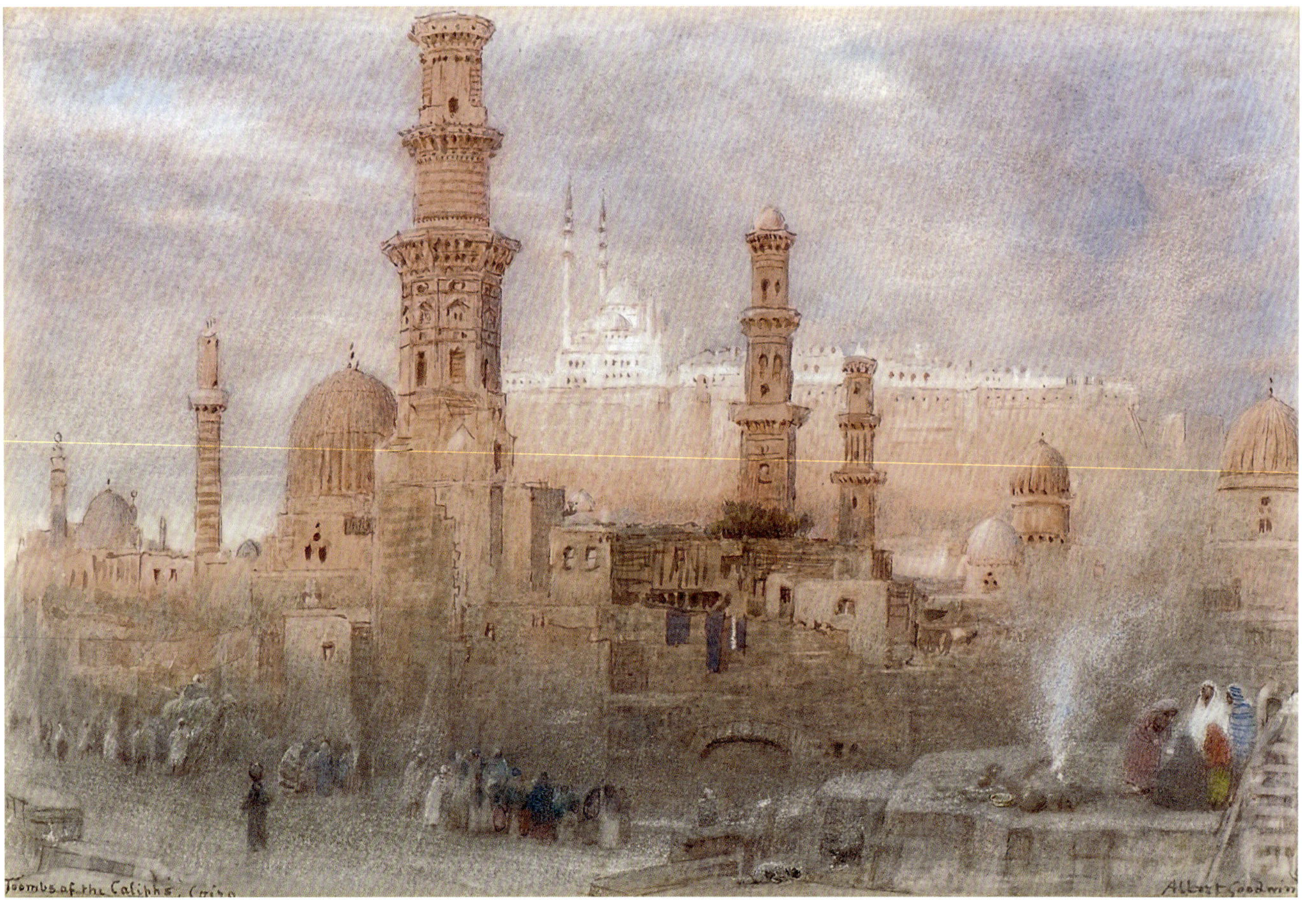

21 **Tombs of the Caliphs, Cairo** (opposite)
Signed, inscribed 'Toombs of the Caliphs, Cairo' and dated /98
Watercolour
10 x 14 ½ inches
Literature:
Albert Goodwin RWS, 1845-1932, London: Chris Beetles Ltd, 1986, Limited Edition of 1000, Plate 60
Exhibited:
Royal Society of Painters in Water-colours, Summer 1898, no 88;
'A Collection of Pictures and Sketches including a series of Whitby and "The First Christmas Dawn" by Albert Goodwin, RWS', Fine Art Society, London, December 1898, no 37;
'Albert Goodwin RWS 1845-1932', Bolton Museum and Art Gallery, August-September 1981, and touring to Canterbury, Newcastle upon Tyne, Leicester and Sotheby's Belgravia, 1981-82, No 94

22 **Jumna Musjid, Agra, Dawn** (below)
Signed and inscribed with title
Watercolour with bodycolour and ink
7 x 9 ¾ inches
Exhibited: 'An Exhibition of Pictures and Watercolours entitled "In Praise of All The Churches: by Albert Goodwin, RWS', Fine Art Society, London, November 1900, no 31

The Jama Masjid mosque stands opposite the Agra Fort in the centre of Agra, Uttar Pradesh. It was built by Jahanara Begum, Padshah Begum (First Lady) of the Mughal Empire, during the reign of her father, Mughal Emperor Shah Jahan and was one of several imperial projects undertaken to improve Agra, then the capital of the Mughal Empire. Built between 1643-48 it is one of the largest mosques in India and is still in use today.

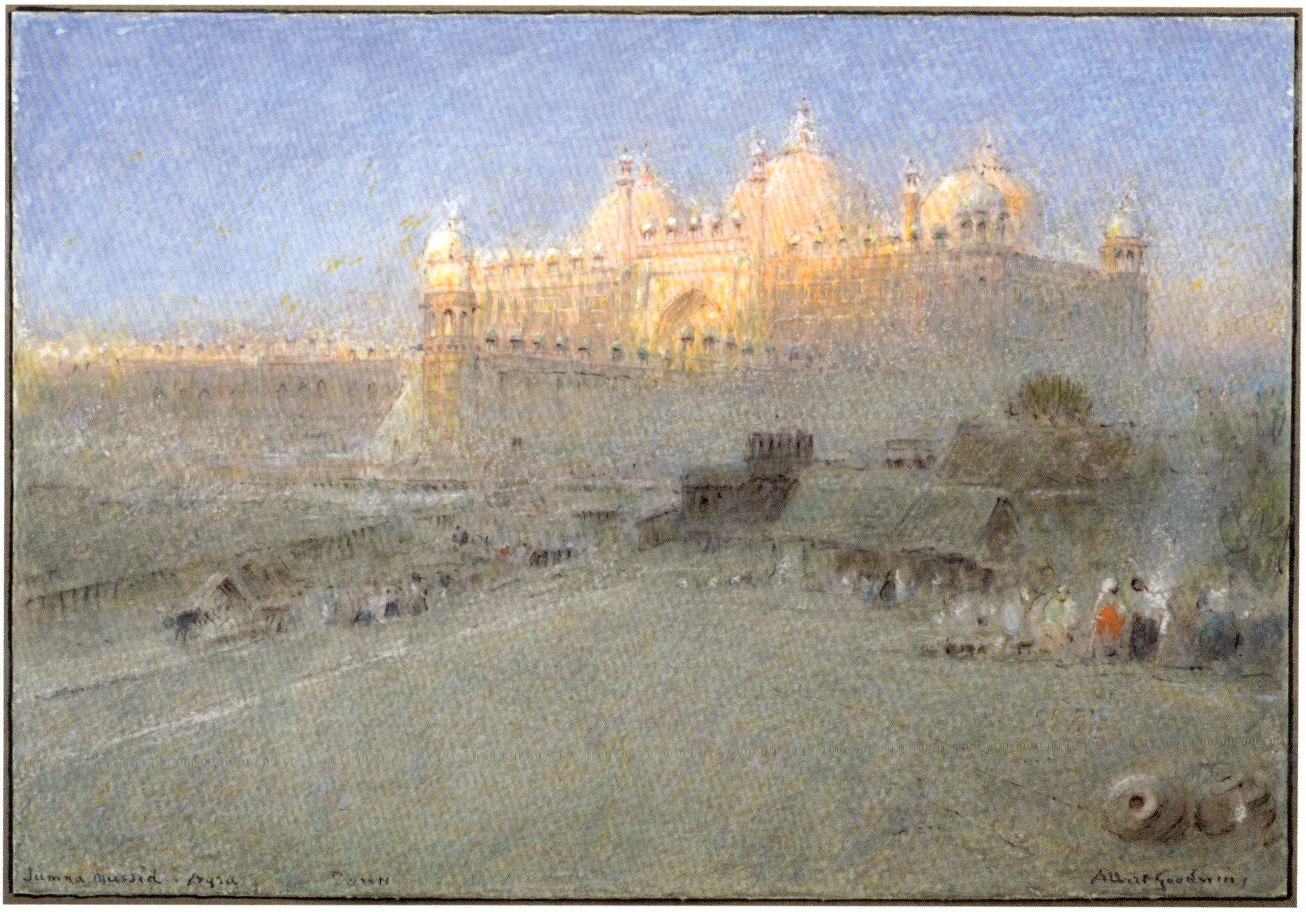

'Allegorical landscape, and still more allegorized landscape painting, is a difficult and particularly uncertain sort of art in which Mr Goodwin, its most accomplished practitioner amongst us, is one of the few who contrive even to approach success. The Source of the Sacred River is almost as suggestive, quite as well painted, and much more understandable. In general it does not differ from a score of similar works by Mr Goodwin, who is not content with painting nature so admirably that few rival him, and leaving to her

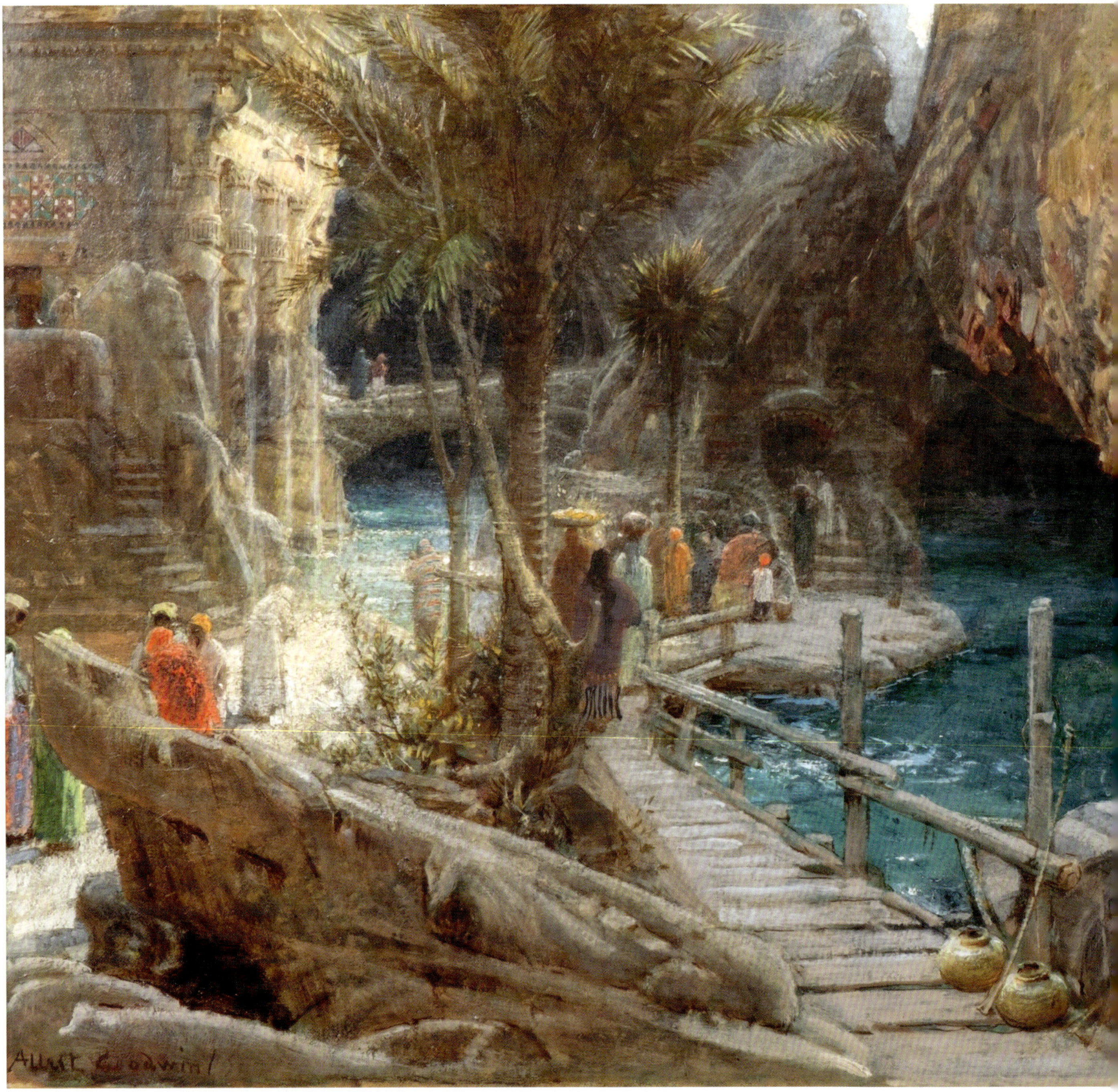

sympathetic lovers the task of recognizing the pathos and poetry which, so to say, harmonizes itself with the spectator's mood. There is nothing to tell us that the stream Mr Goodwin depicted so rarely is sacred in any exceptional sense, but there is much we can be grateful for in its abundant and sumptuous harmonies of colour, form, and light, and the dignity of its masses.'

(*The Athenaeum*, 1900)

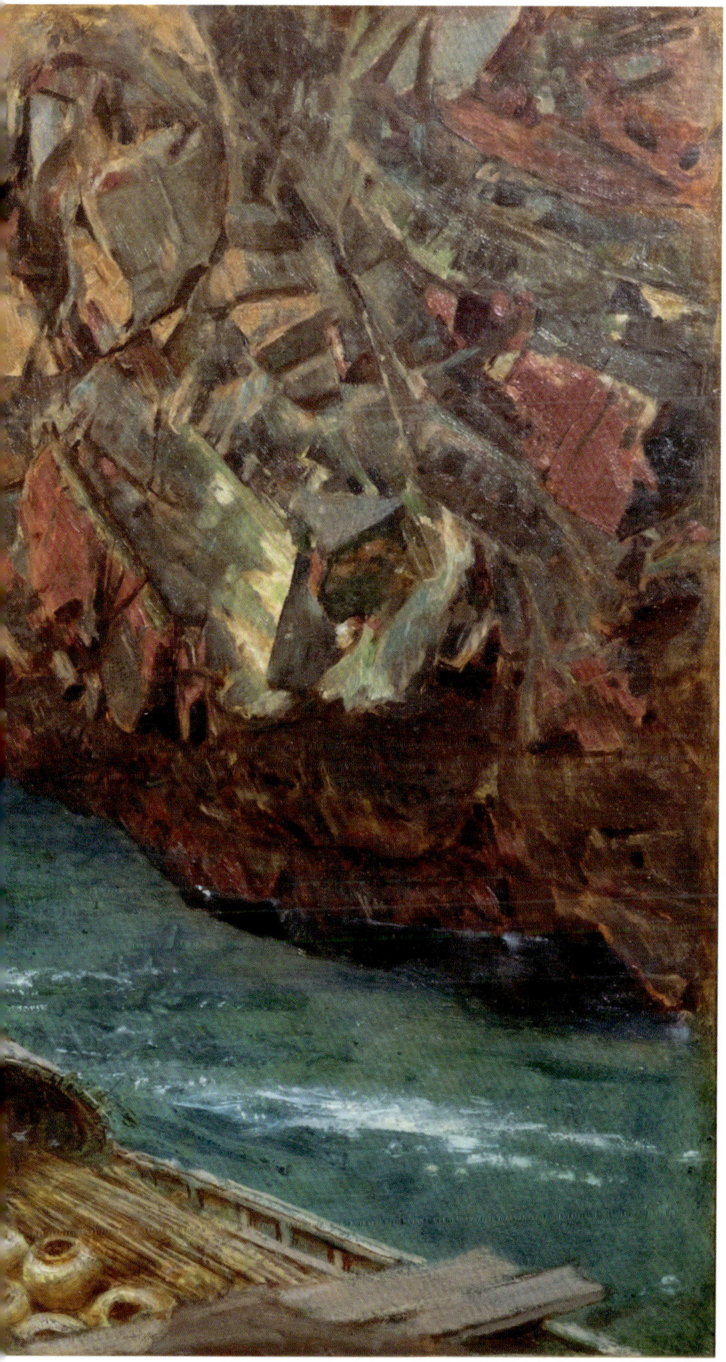

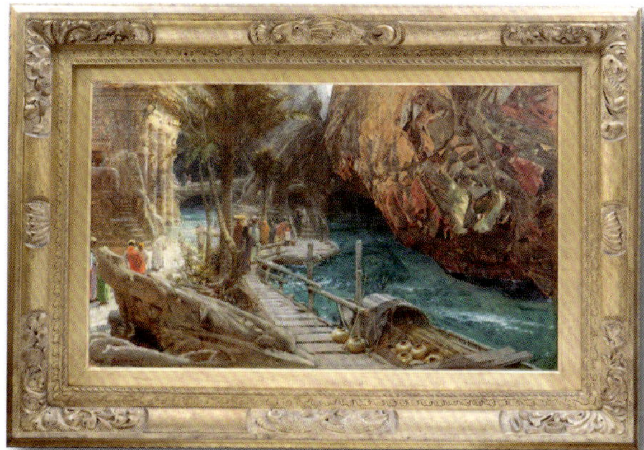

23 **The Source of the Sacred River**
Signed
Signed on label on reverse
Oil on canvas
21 ½ x 35 inches
Literature:
Hammond Smith, *Albert Goodwin RWS*, Leigh-on-Sea: F Lewis, 1977, Plate 51;
Albert Goodwin RWS, 1845-1932, London: Chris Beetles Ltd, 1986, Limited Edition of 1000, Plate 64
Exhibited:
Royal Academy of Arts, 1900, No 463;
'An Exhibition of Pictures and Watercolours entitled "In Praise of All The Churches" by Albert Goodwin, RWS', Fine Art Society, December 1900, no 59;
'Inaugural Exhibition: a Celebration of British & European Painting of the 19th and 20th Centuries', Peter Nahum: Chris Beetles, March 1985, page 53;
A Museum Tour of the Royal Watercolour Society, Sheffield Mappin Art Gallery, Ruskin Gallery, Stoke on Trent City Museum and Art Gallery, May-October 1986, No 11

In original carved, gilded oak frame by Charles Goodwin.

The source of the River Ganges, which is regarded by the Hindu population of India as sacred, is at Lapthal, in the Himalayas on the frontier between India and China.

'Starting for West Indies as guest of Arthur McConnell together with Edytha, to return by U.S.A. seeing Niagara A.B.W.

How much hangs on that A.B.W.? Have left my work ready for R.W.S. and R.A., so nothing doth hinder from that point of view and the rest from the ceaseless anxiety of Picture-making, is a very present blessing. We are bound first for Barbados, there to cruise in among the Islands, then to stay a week in Demerara and a month in Jamaica, after that to see something of Canada, Niagara, and the possibility of getting as far as Quebec before returning in May.'

(*The Diary of Albert Goodwin, RWS, 1883-1927*, Privately Printed, 1934, Page 41, 22 January 1902, First visit to West Indies, On board W.I.M.S. 'Trent' – off Isle of Wight)

'St Vincent we reached at dawn — a very striking one. Got up at 4.30 a.m. — my berth so intolerably hot and the other man in the other berth having so fearful a snore that he appeared to be trying all he could to burst himself. I got up at 12 and lay down in the saloon, where I managed, with the tablecloth for a pillow, to get a snatch or two of unconsciousness. St Vincent was half hidden in dark rainclouds and mist, very suggestive of volcanic eruptions — it has a history of that kind — a still smoking crater or lake which boils in the mountains. We only had two hours there, and then on to Grenada, where we had time enough o go ashore and see the rather quaint little place and to make my first acquaintance with the land "crab." a most ludicrous creature. They looked like large pink and red leaves lying about, which strangely rolled away into holes as we came near. It was not till two or three seemed to be sucked down that I realized they were living things with generally one eye left up atop of their hole to watch the movements of the enemy!

Sunstroky hot. I was most grateful to my own self for my kind thought of myself in getting me a panama hat at Barbados. He who goes out without one or a sun-hat in this climate is making a covenant with death!'

(*The Diary of Albert Goodwin, RWS, 1883-1927*, Privately Printed, 1934, Page 41, 4 February 1902, Off Grenada)

24 **Jungle, The Explorers**
Signed and inscribed 'Jungle'
Inscribed 'The Explorers' below mount
Watercolour and bodycolour
10 ½ x 15 inches
Exhibited: Possibly the painting exhibited in Royal Society of Painters in Water-Colours, Spring 1910, No 144 as 'The Jungle'

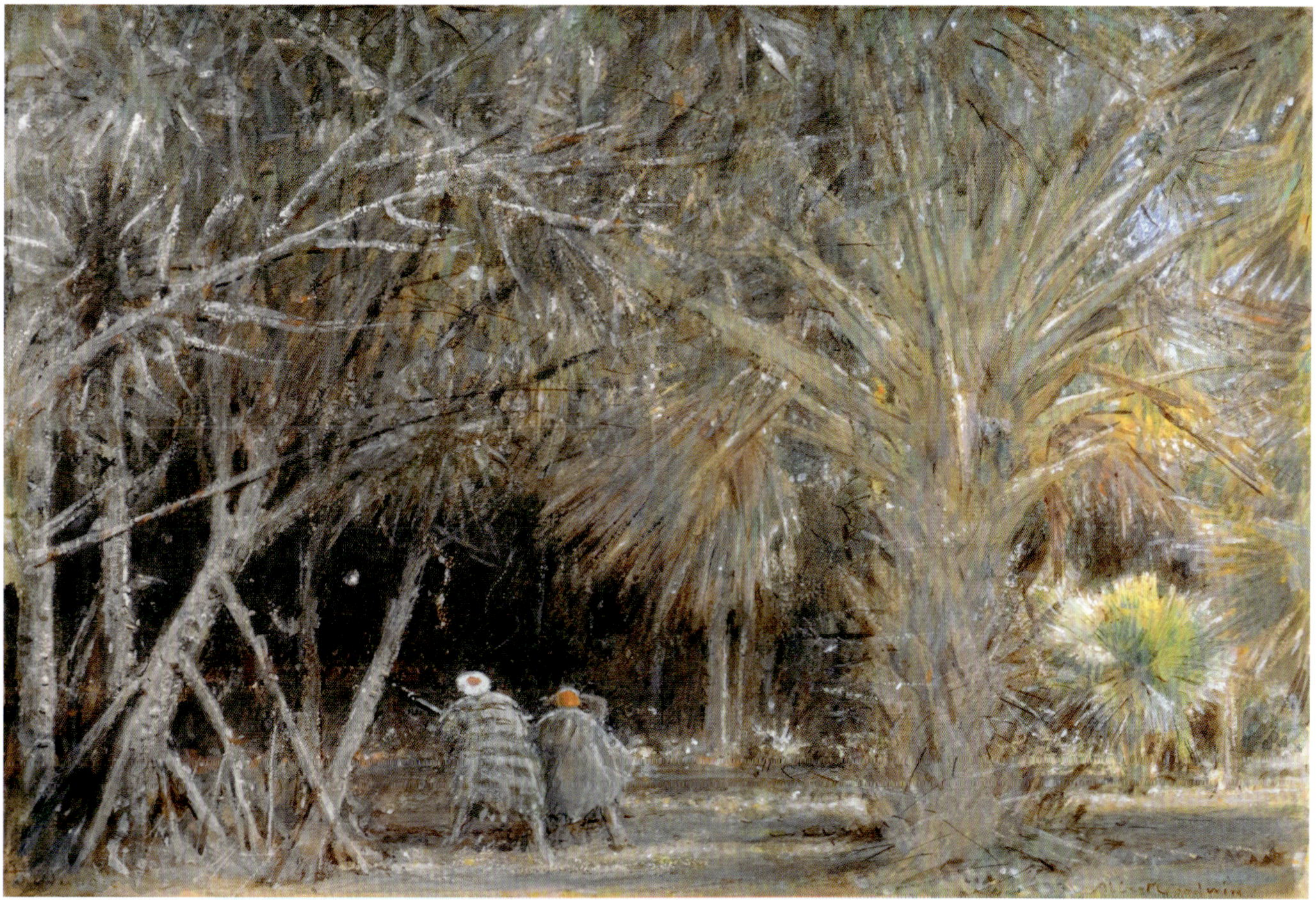

'We to the place have come, where I have told thee
Thou shalt behold the people dolorous
Who have forgone the good of intellect.

'My Son' the courteous Master said to me,
'All those who perish in the wrath of God
Here meet together out of every land'

(Dante's 'Inferno')

'I think I had more trouble in developing this, than any picture I have painted, but the agony (and some one has said somewhere, nothing good without agony) had its reward. There is great joy in creating even if it is the counterfeit presentment of so awesome a place. Some of the prisoners have carved on the walls of this prison-house as they entered, words which speak of more merciful things that Dante wrote of. It is from that wide point of view, I think, that Hell becomes as reasonable as Heaven.

Some parts of India and some of the Cyclopean rock-carving of Upper Egypt gave me the impression for the foundation of the haunting subject. They seemed the nearest I had seen to the dreadfulness of this Dante story.'

(Albert Goodwin's note to the exhibition of this painting at the Leggatt Brothers' Gallery exhibition, 1908.)

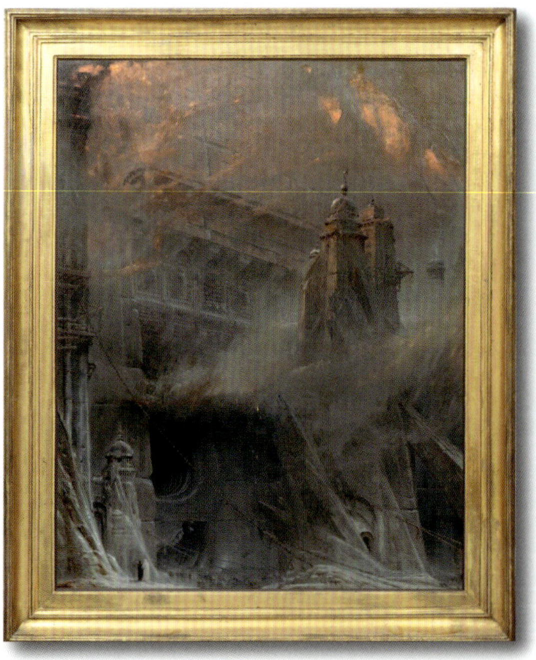

25 **The Gate of the Inferno**
Signed and inscribed with title
Signed and inscribed 'The Gate of the Inferno. Through me the way among the people lost. By Dante's Inferno. Albert Goodwin, 7 Mount Terrace, Ilfracombe' on label on stretcher
Oil on canvas
55 ½ x 41 ¼ inches
Exhibited:
Royal Academy of Arts, 1903, No 304;
'Drawings and Pictures by Albert Goodwin, RWS', Leggatt Brothers' Gallery, London, 1908, no 47

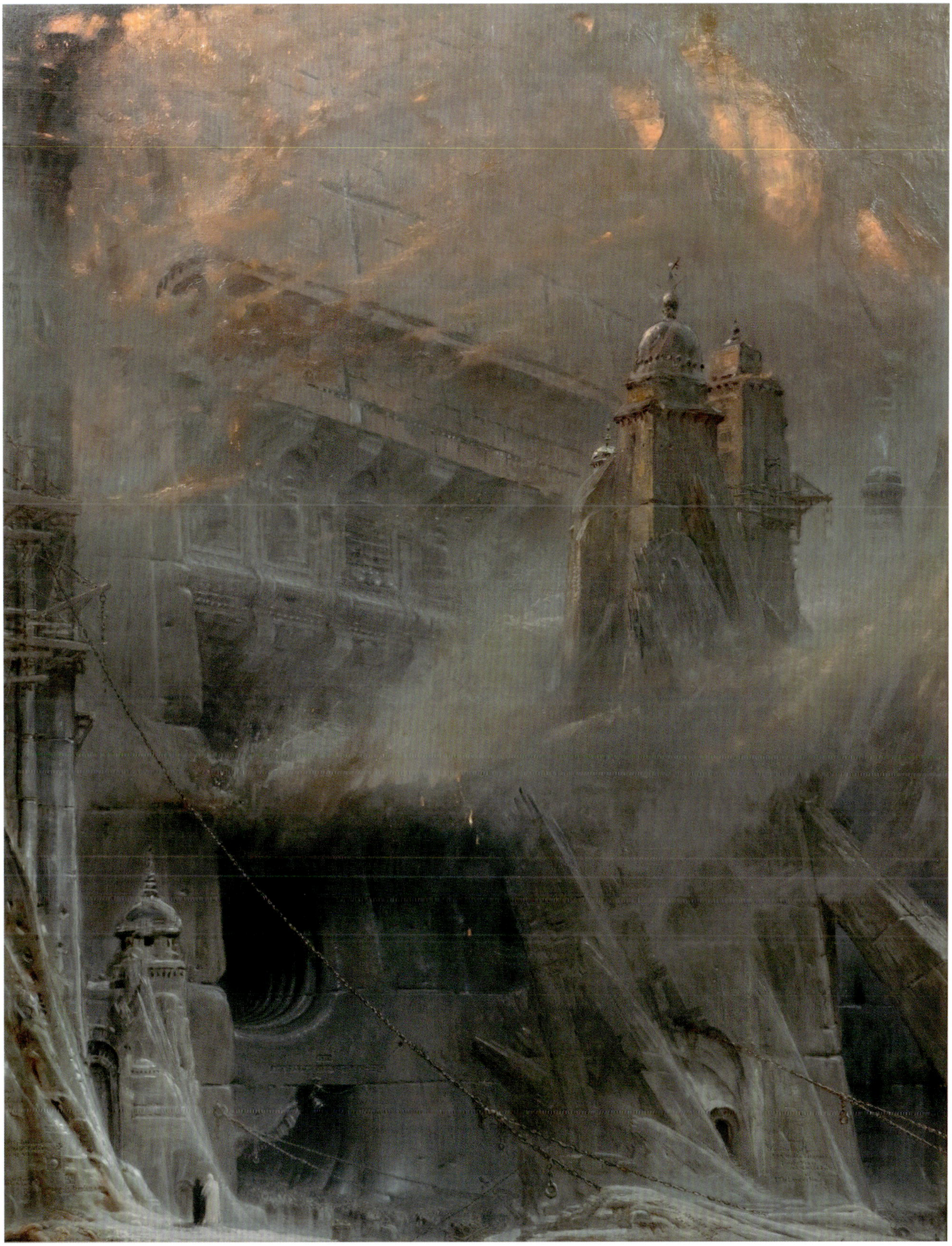

26 **Venezia**
Signed, inscribed with title and dated 1901
Watercolour with bodycolour
23 ½ x 60 inches
Provenance:
H J Cornish, 1928
Literature:
Hammond Smith, *Albert Goodwin RWS*, Leigh on Sea: F Lewis, 1977, Plate 1
Exhibited:
Royal Society of Painters in Water-Colours, Summer 1902, No 53 as 'Venice';
'Chris Beetles Summer Show', Chris Beetles Gallery, London, 2001, No 35

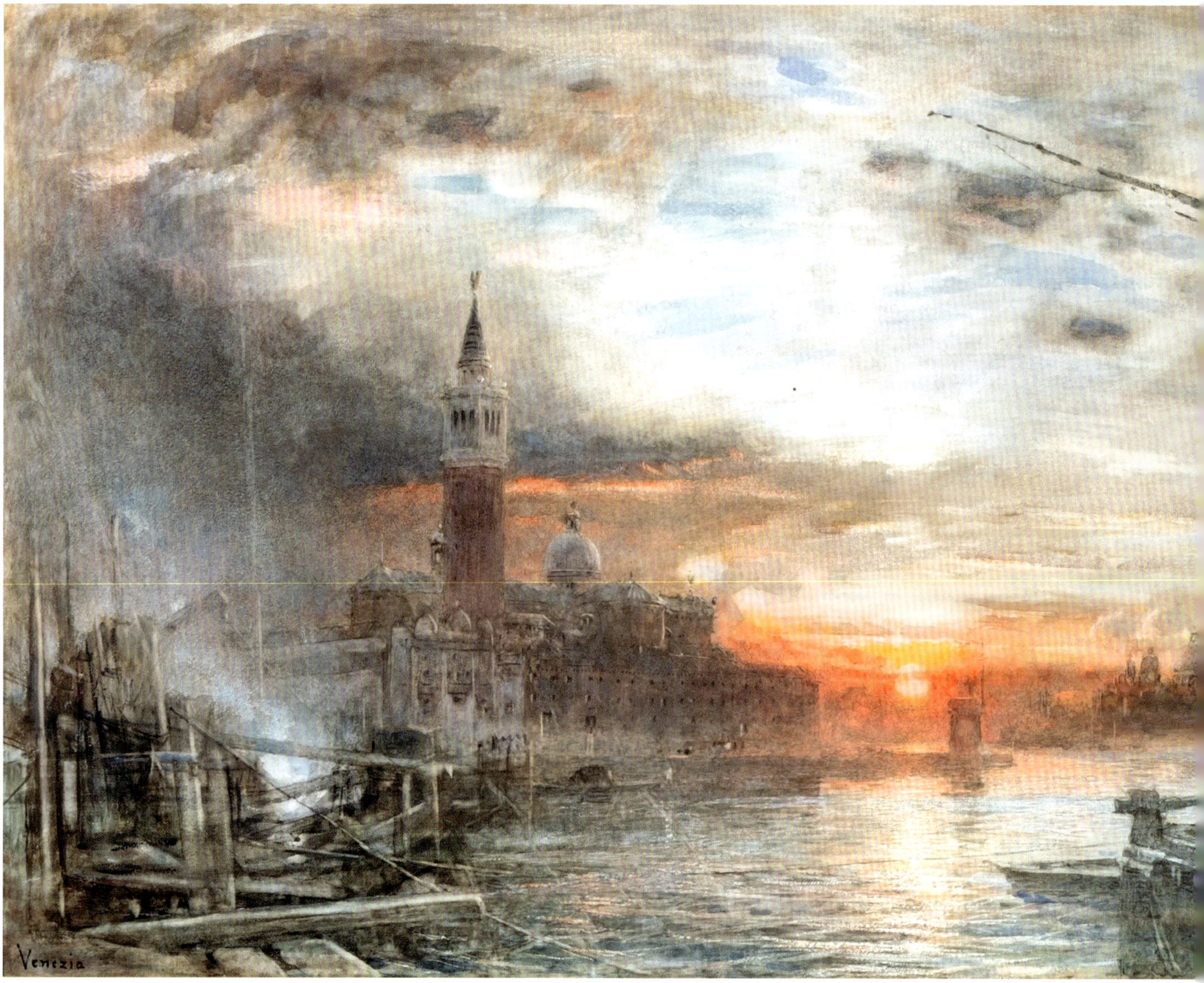

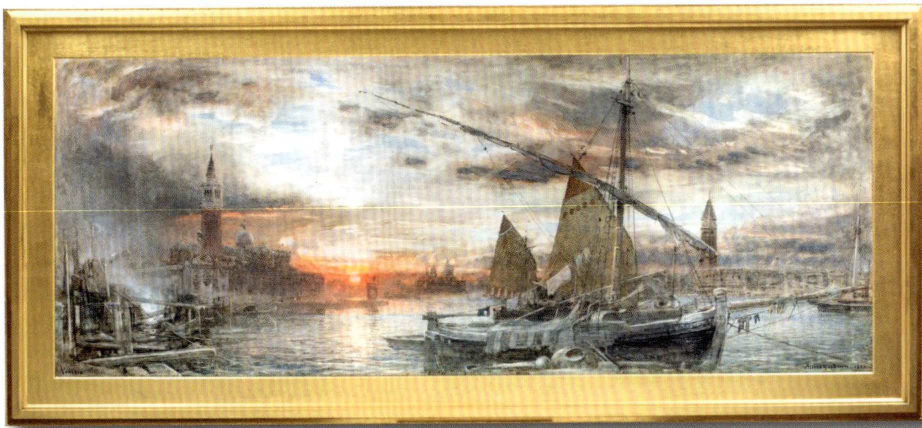

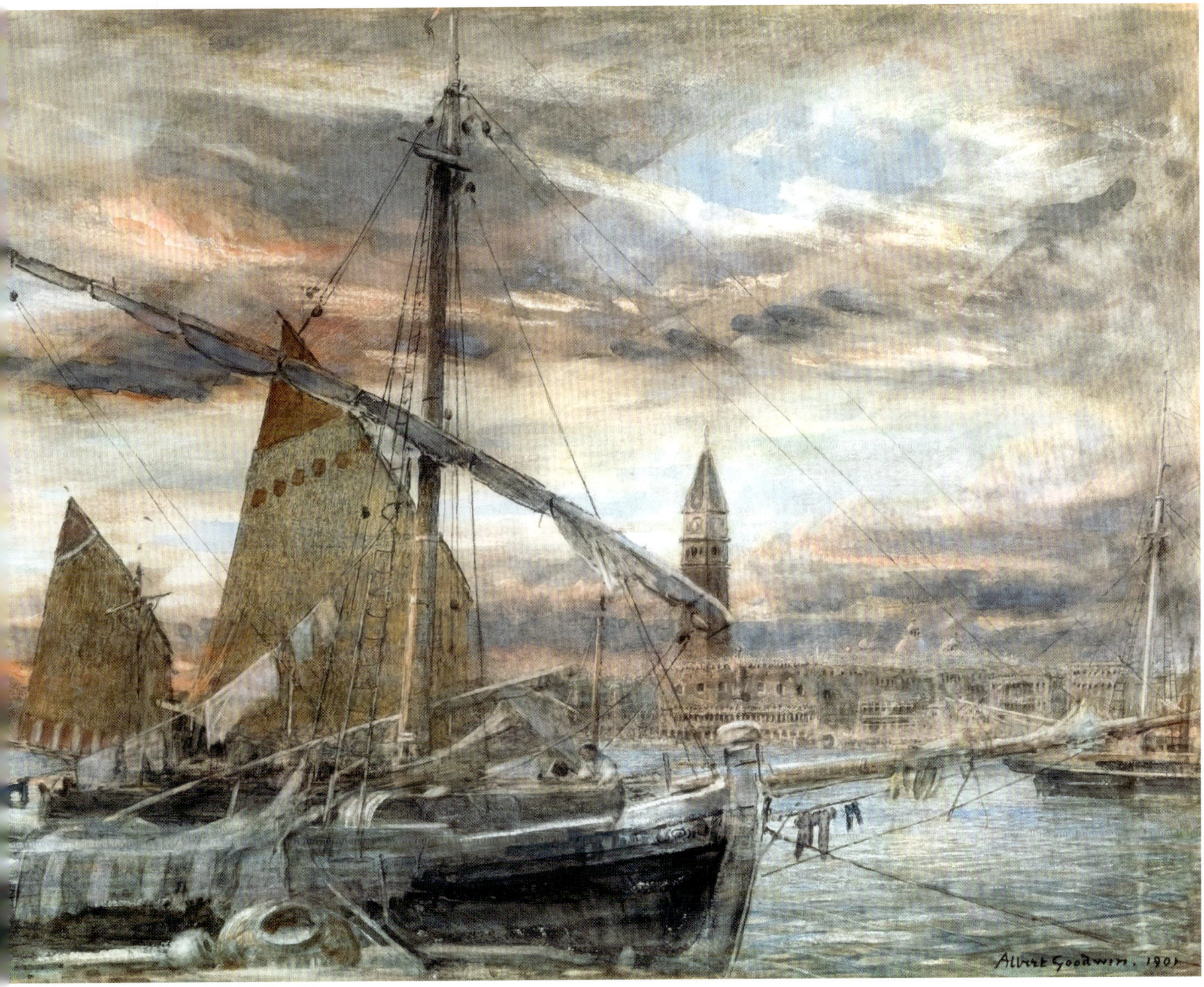
Albert Goodwin. 1901

'Will there be anything more wonderful than the higher Alps in the Kingdom of Heaven'

(*The Diary of Albert Goodwin, RWS, 1883-1927*, Privately Printed, 1934, Page 371, 29 November 1917)

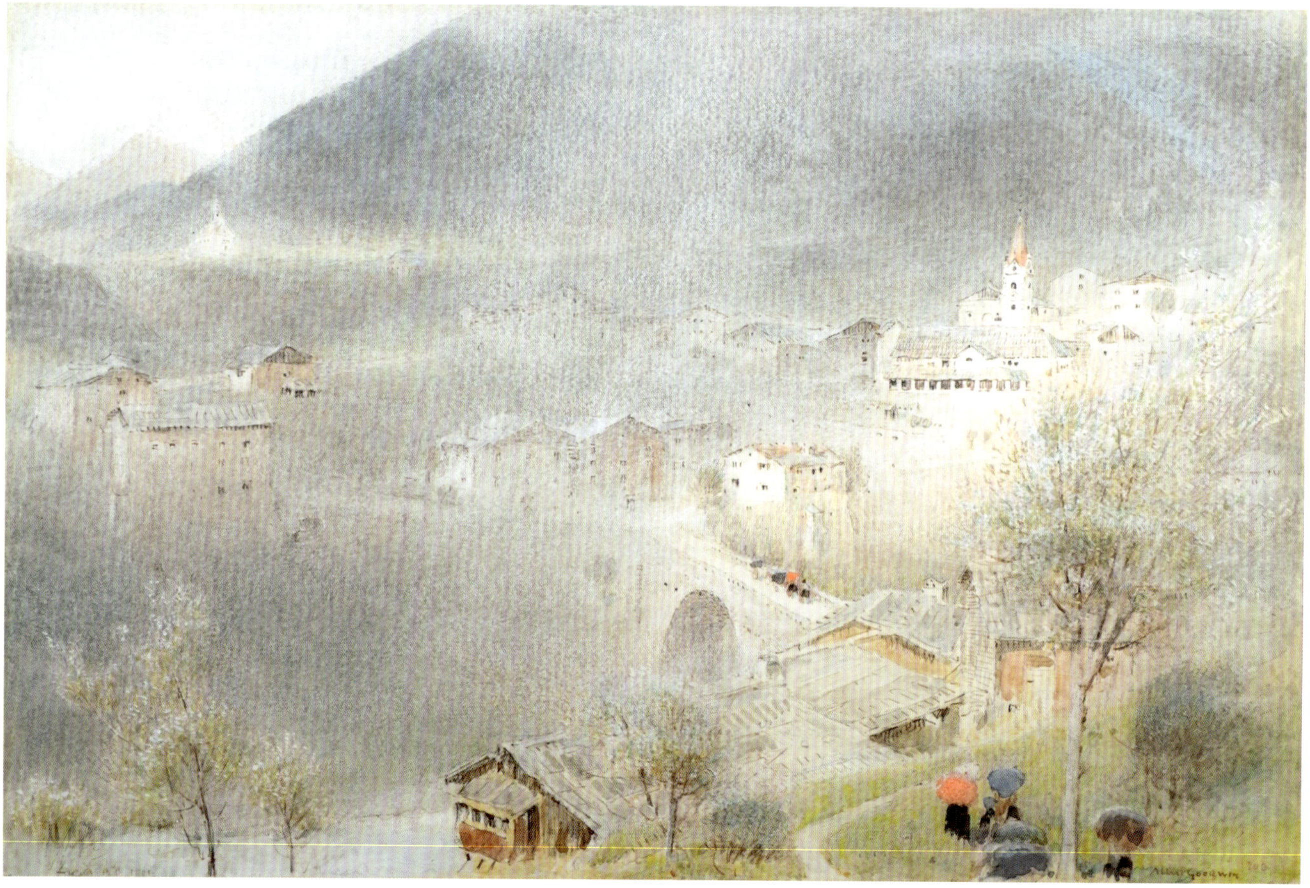

27 **Swiss View**
Signed and dated 1908 and 'August 28 1904'
Watercolour
10 x 14 ¾ inches

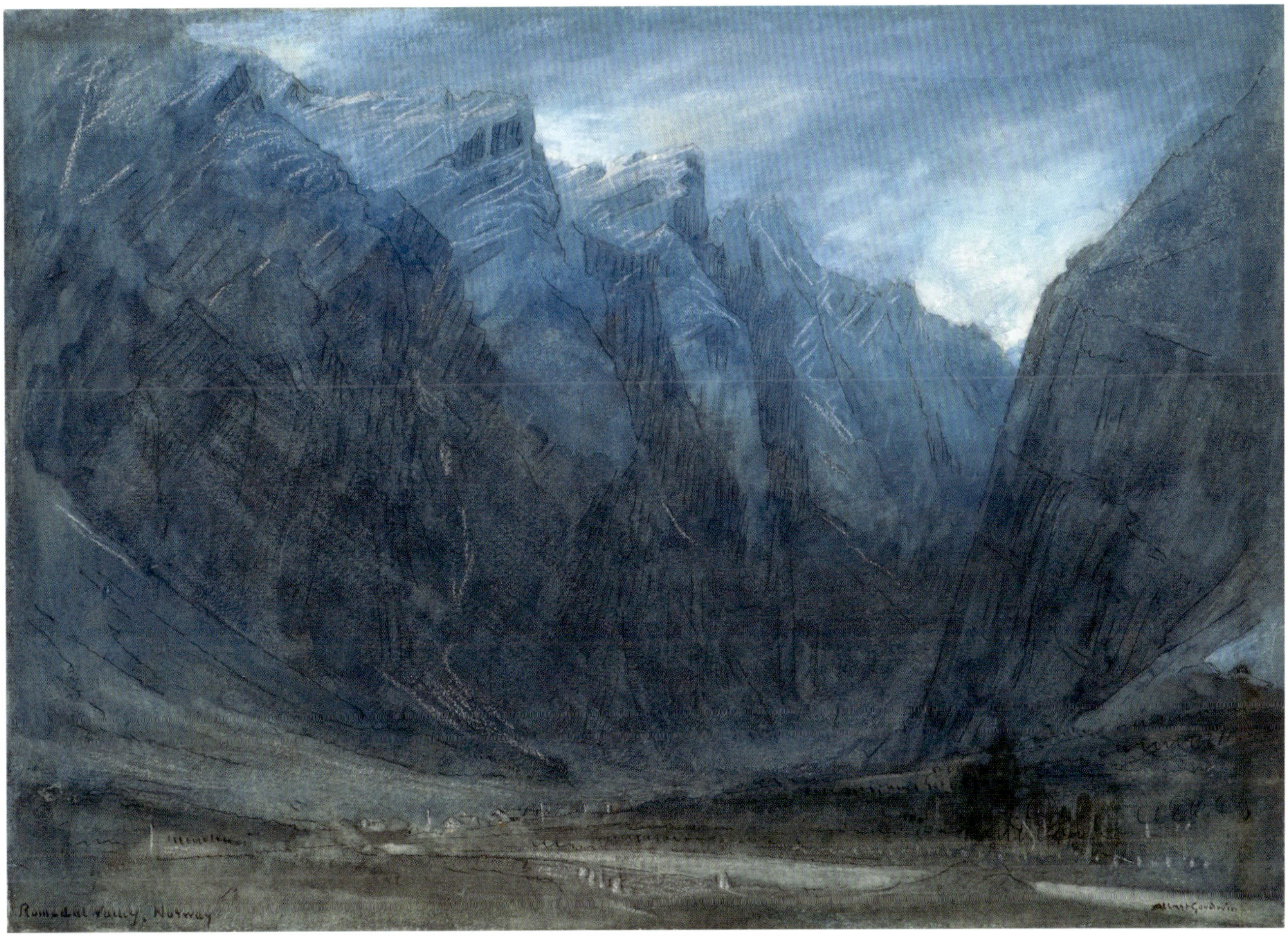

28 Romsdal Valley, Norway
Signed and inscribed with title
Watercolour with bodycolour, chalk and ink
11 x 15 inches
Exhibited:
'Albert Goodwin RWS 1845-1932', Bolton Museum and Art Gallery, August-September 1981, and touring to Canterbury, Newcastle upon Tyne, Leicester and Sotheby's Belgravia, 1981-82, No 87

Albert Goodwin visited Norway in 1892

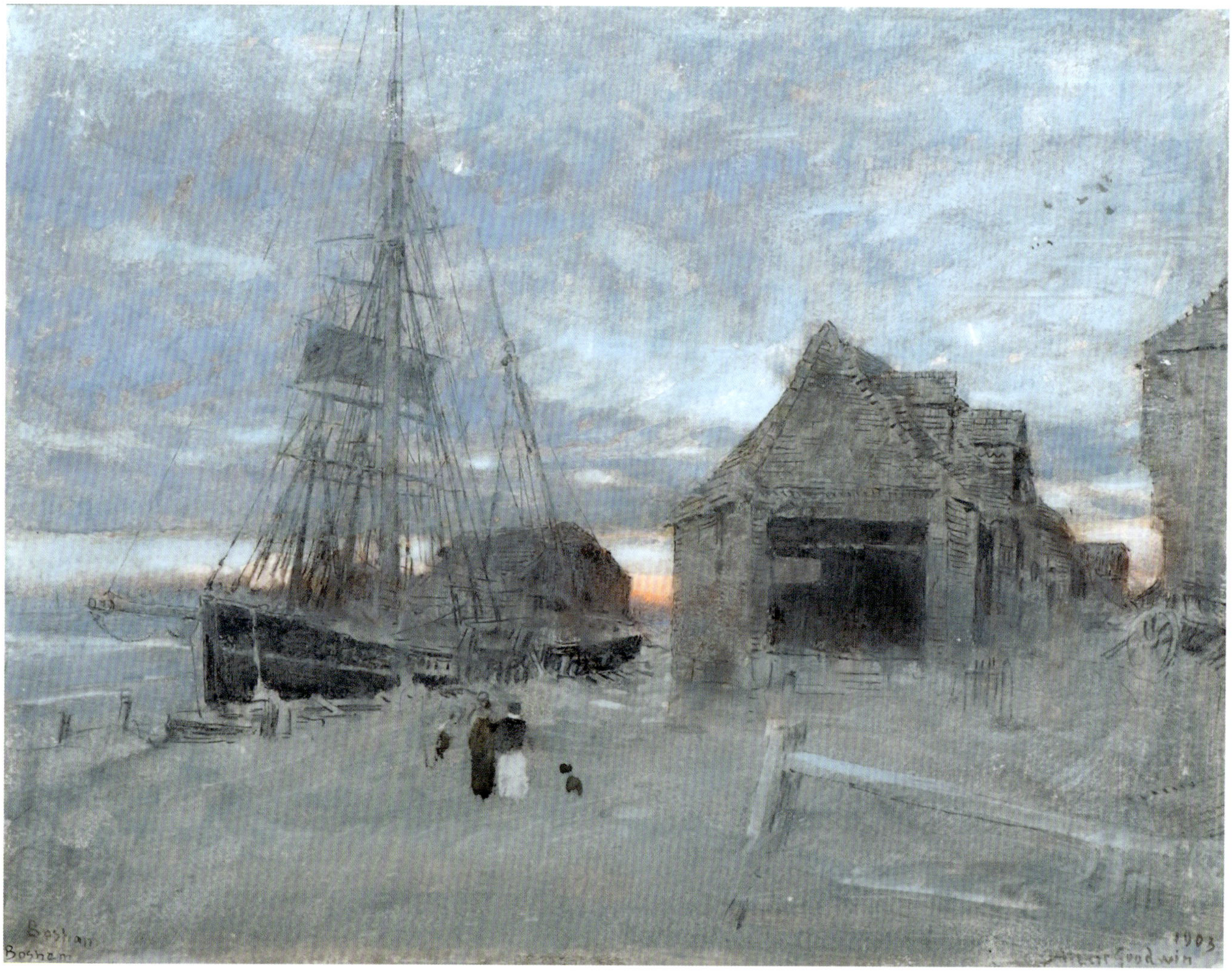

29 **Bosham**
Signed, inscribed with title twice and dated 1903
Watercolour and bodycolour
9 ¾ x 12 ¼ inches
Exhibited:
'Water Colour Drawings by Albert Goodwin, RWS', Robert Dunthorne's
The Rembrandt Head Gallery, 1904, No 37;
Albert Goodwin, RWS (1845-1932), Chris Beetles Gallery, June 2007, No 77

'Mr Goodwin's mannerisms are rather exceptionally pronounced this year, and among six or seven works, beautiful as they all are, there is nothing quite as good as the "Salisbury" of a year or two ago. He has however, a fine "Siena", and for his principal work, a highly poetical "Pompeii by Moonlight"'

(*The Times*, 11 April, 1904, Society of Painters in Watercolours)

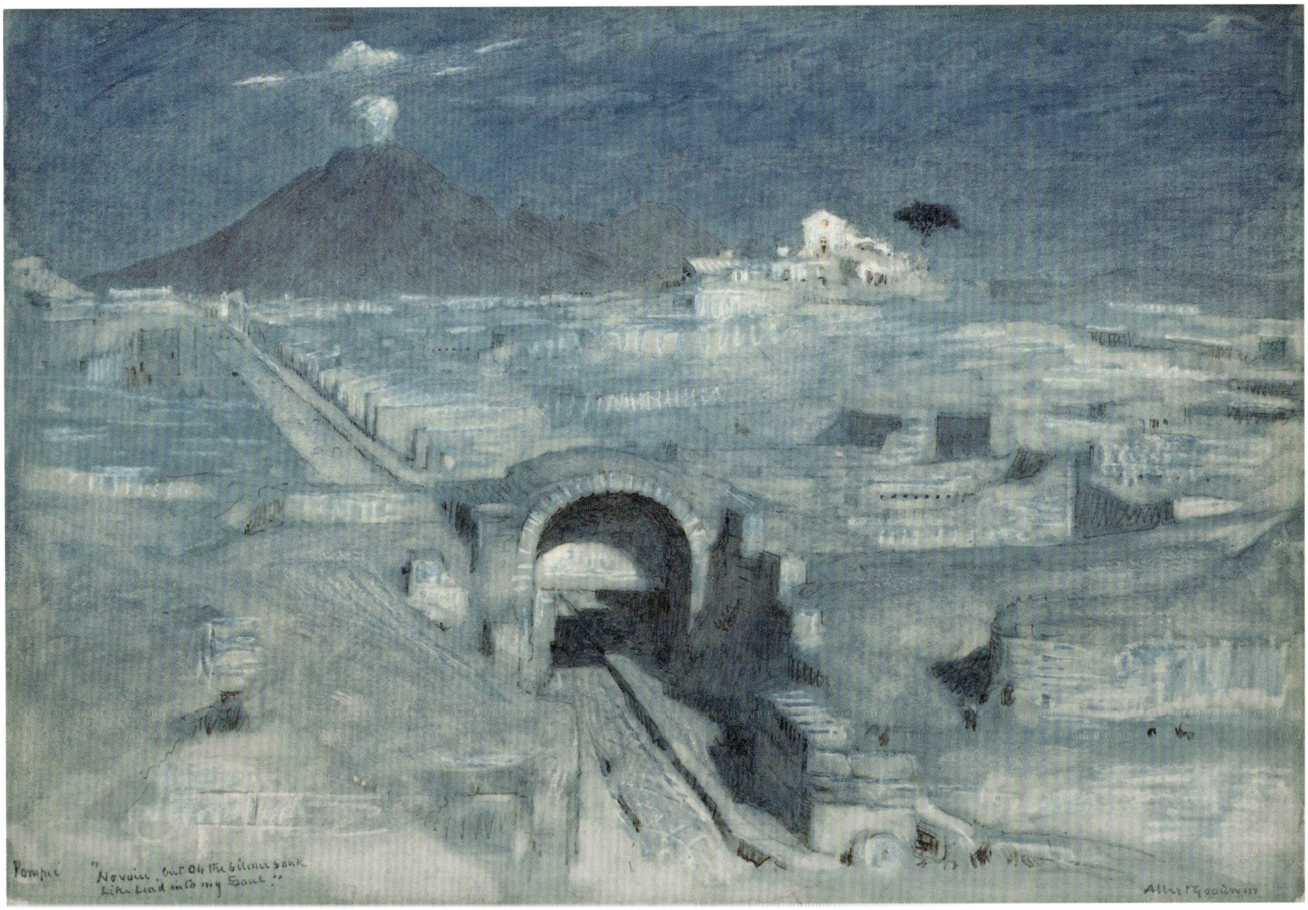

30 Pompei "No voice, but Oh the silence sank with lead into my Soul."
Signed and inscribed with title
Watercolour with bodycolour and ink
10 ½ x 14 ¾ inches
Literature:
Albert Goodwin RWS, 1845-1932, London: Chris Beetles Ltd, 1986, Limited Edition of 1000, Plate 85 (larger version)
Exhibited:
Royal Society of Painters in Watercolour, Summer 1904, no 111 (larger version)
Preliminary drawing for the larger painting entitled 'A Silent Highway, Pompeii.
"How Doth the City Sit Solitary that was Full of People.", exhibited at the Royal Society of Painters in Water-colours, Summer 1904, No 111

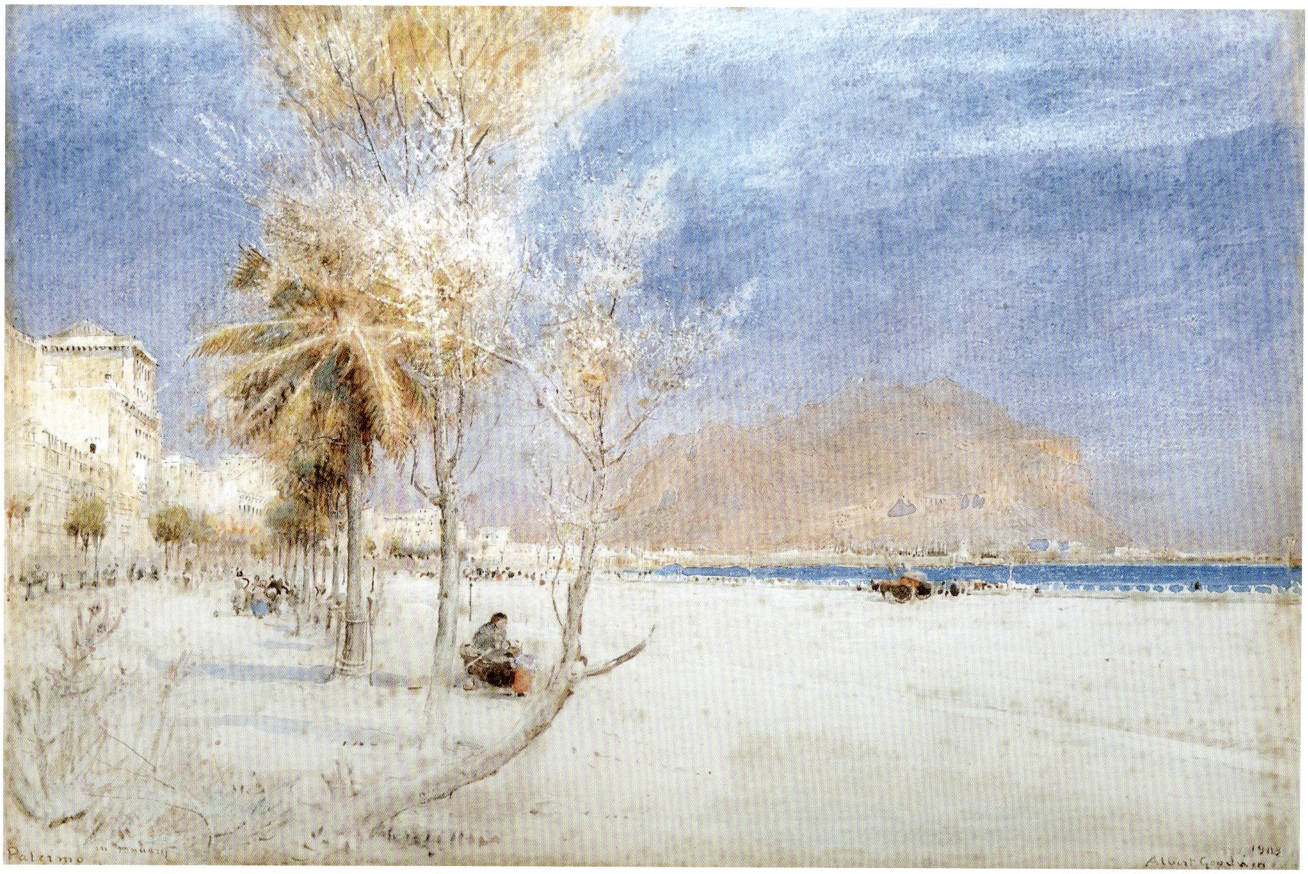

31 **Palermo in January**
Signed, inscribed with title and dated 1903
Watercolour
10 x 14 ½ inches
Exhibited: 'A Collection of Water-Colour Drawings by Albert Goodwin, RWS',
Robert Dunthorne's The Rembrandt Gallery, London, 1904, no 23

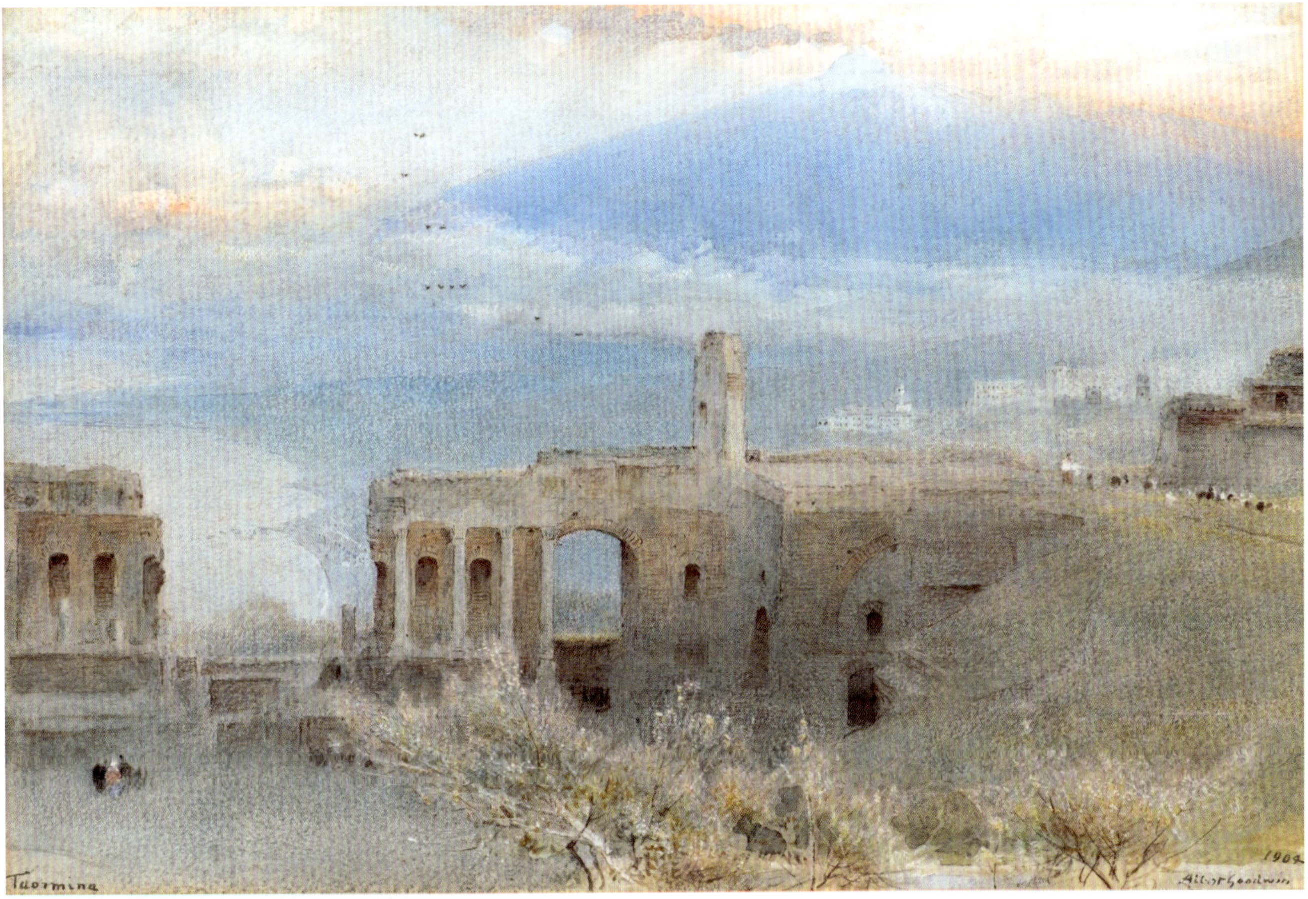

32 **Taormina**
Signed, inscribed with title and dated 1904
Signed with initials below mount
Watercolour
10 x 14 ¾ inches

'Came here, after much searching after "Apartments" in Berwick-on-Tweed. Here we have at last settled in this little "furnished house" and with great restfulness of content. A most delightful, unspoilt village, with some of the scarlet Whitby tiles in it, and a most interesting country round about. Biked into Cley last evening to find it a picturesque village with something almost magnificent in its church! The weather is perfect, day after day the same cloudless sky and this for nearly a week now: much to be thankful for once again. Three days' stay in York, under the Cathedral: from the windows of bedroom, the Minster looked very impressive, expecially in the twilight. Managed to get an outline, which to-day I am painting - though I suppose I ought to be out of doors! Glad to find I had not altogether lost the power of outline: for pastel is, I see, somewhat liable to demoralize the severity of form and one needs to hark back to the black and white for personal safety! How much of Impressionism is another excuse for "scamping" both form and detail? The analogy seems to come in that a lot of so-called Agnosticism is another name for laziness in thinking. Though the tyranny of much of that is now overpast. But with Carlyle as its champion and defender Froude, and Ruskin – for he, for a long while, was under this cloud - and a good many others at one time, it was a real tyranny. Now one can see, to some extent, to the back of it, and see the god they set up was a very little one: a god, who having made his world, was not going to trouble; an impressionist in fact, who was a fairly good generalizer, but was not going to trouble himself about mere details!'

(*The Diary of Albert Goodwin, RWS, 1883-1927*, Privately Printed, 1934, Page 117, August 17 or 18? 1909, Weybourne, Norfolk)

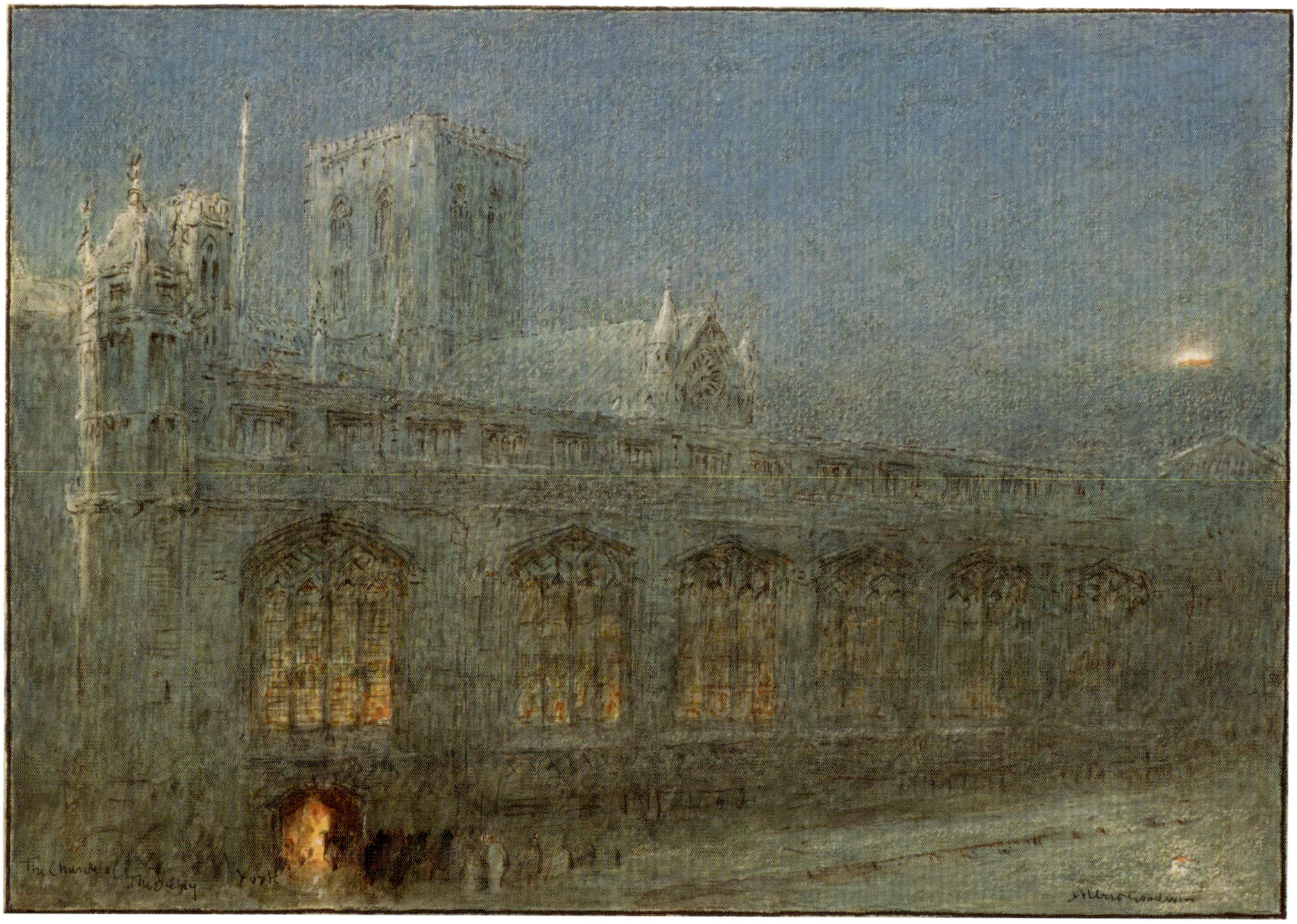

33 **The Church of the Belfry, York** (opposite)
Signed and inscribed with title
Watercolour
11 x 15 ¼ inches
Literature:
Albert Goodwin RWS, 1845-1932, London: Chris Beetles, 1986,
Limited Edition of 1000, Plate 114
Exhibited:
A Museum Tour of the Royal Watercolour Society,
Sheffield Mappin Art Gallery, Ruskin Gallery, Stoke on Trent City
Museum and Art Gallery, May-October 1986, No 75

34 **Canterbury Cathedral. A Soldiers' Parade** (below)
Signed and inscribed 'Canterbury'
Watercolour with ink
10 ¼ x 14 ½ inches
Literature:
The Studio Vol LXXIII, No 301, Page 83, 'Albert Goodwin RWS'
by Sir Frederick Wedmore;
Albert Goodwin RWS, 1845-1932, London: Chris Beetles Ltd, 1986,
Limited Edition of 1000, Plate 86

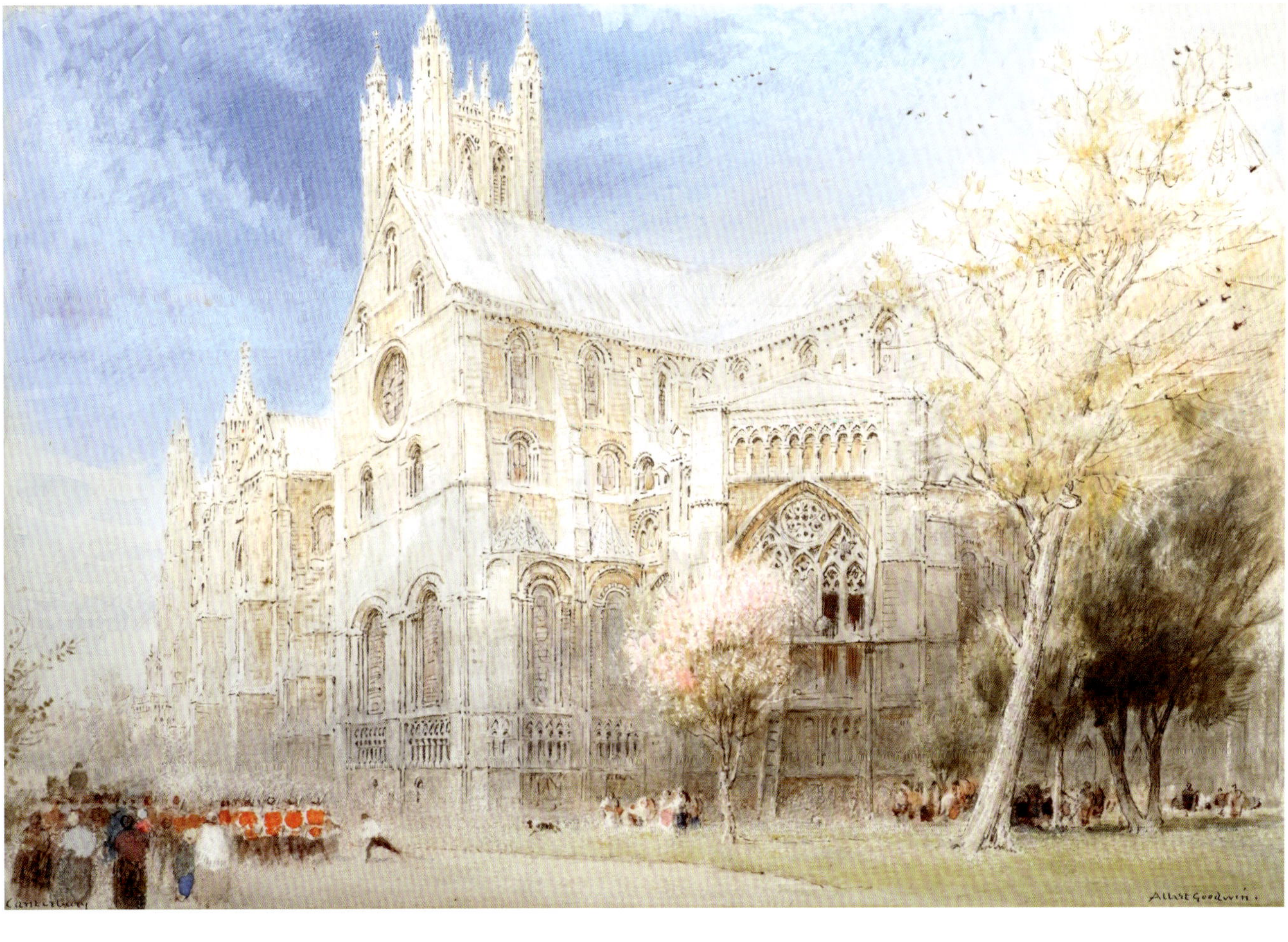

'Sent for tickets for Baveno, for the four of us to start on Friday next. Went over to Winchelsea and got a note for some sketches of Rye and Winchelsea, wanted to illustrate an article in "Studio": fortunately I have most of them ready, as they are wanted at once.'

'After all, had to go to London, partly to take up some drawings for reproduction in the "Studio" – six of which are to be done.'

(*The Diary of Albert Goodwin, RWS, 1883-1927*, Privately Printed, 1934, Page 111, 19 & 21 April, 1909)

'Herbert Marshall and Albert Goodwin are amongst those who have made these towns their own, and amonst the latter's most beautiful drawings must be counted some red Cinque Port of Rye. Both it and Winchelsea possess good inns for artists, although the "Mermaid" at the former has now been taken possession of by golfers, who threaten to oust the painter from what was once looked upon as his peculiar possession. There are other towns in Sussex which retain much of their eighteenth-century character, but Rye carries one back much further than that, and it is a mediaeval town that you come upon as you enter the old gateways, both here and at Winchelsea. As regards the first named, subjects abound, both of its streets and of the town and harbour from the flats.'

(Marcus Huish, *The Studio*, Special Summer Number, 'Sketching Grounds', 1909)

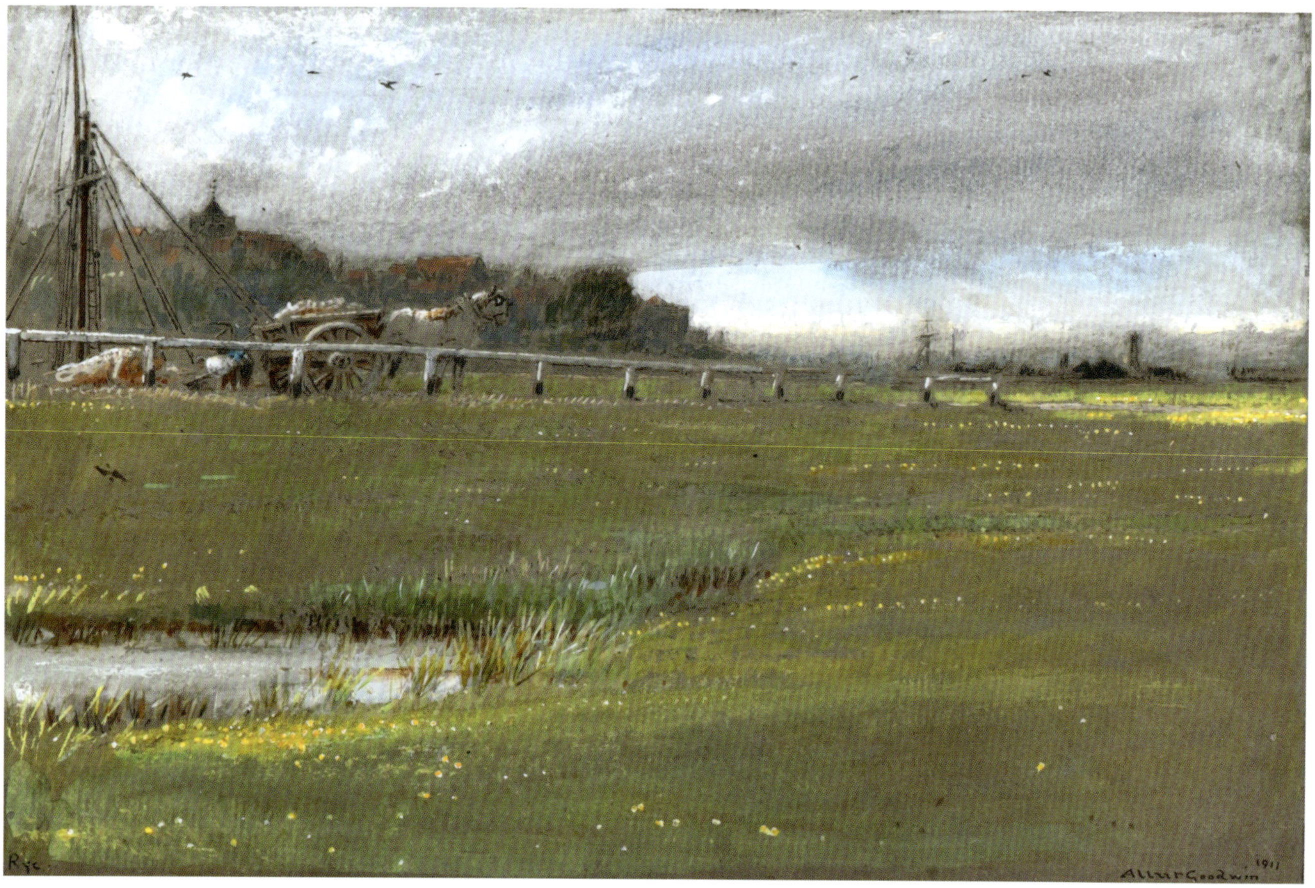

35 **Rye** (opposite)
Signed, inscribed with title and dated 1911
Watercolour, bodycolour, ink and pencil on tinted paper
10 x 14 ¾ inches

36 **The Tares. Poppies in Corn. Salisbury** (below)
Signed, inscribed with title and dated 'July 1907'
Watercolour
18 ½ x 25 inches
Literature:
Albert Goodwin RWS, 1845-1932, London: Chris Beetles Ltd, 1986, Limited Edition of 1000, Plate 102
Exhibited:
'Albert Goodwin RWS 1845-1932', Bolton Museum and Art Gallery, August-September 1981,
and touring to Canterbury, Newcastle upon Tyne, Leicester and Sotheby's Belgravia, 1981-82, No 30;
Albert Goodwin RWS 1845-1932. 129 of His Best Works Borrowed From Private Collections.
A Museum Tour of the Royal Watercolour Society, Sheffield Mappin Art Gallery, Ruskin Gallery,
Stoke on Trent City Museum and Art Gallery, May-October 1986, No 70;
'A Watercolourist's Dream. Albert Goodwin (1845-1932) & John Lewis Roget (1828-1908)',
The County Gallery, Maidstone, February-March 1999

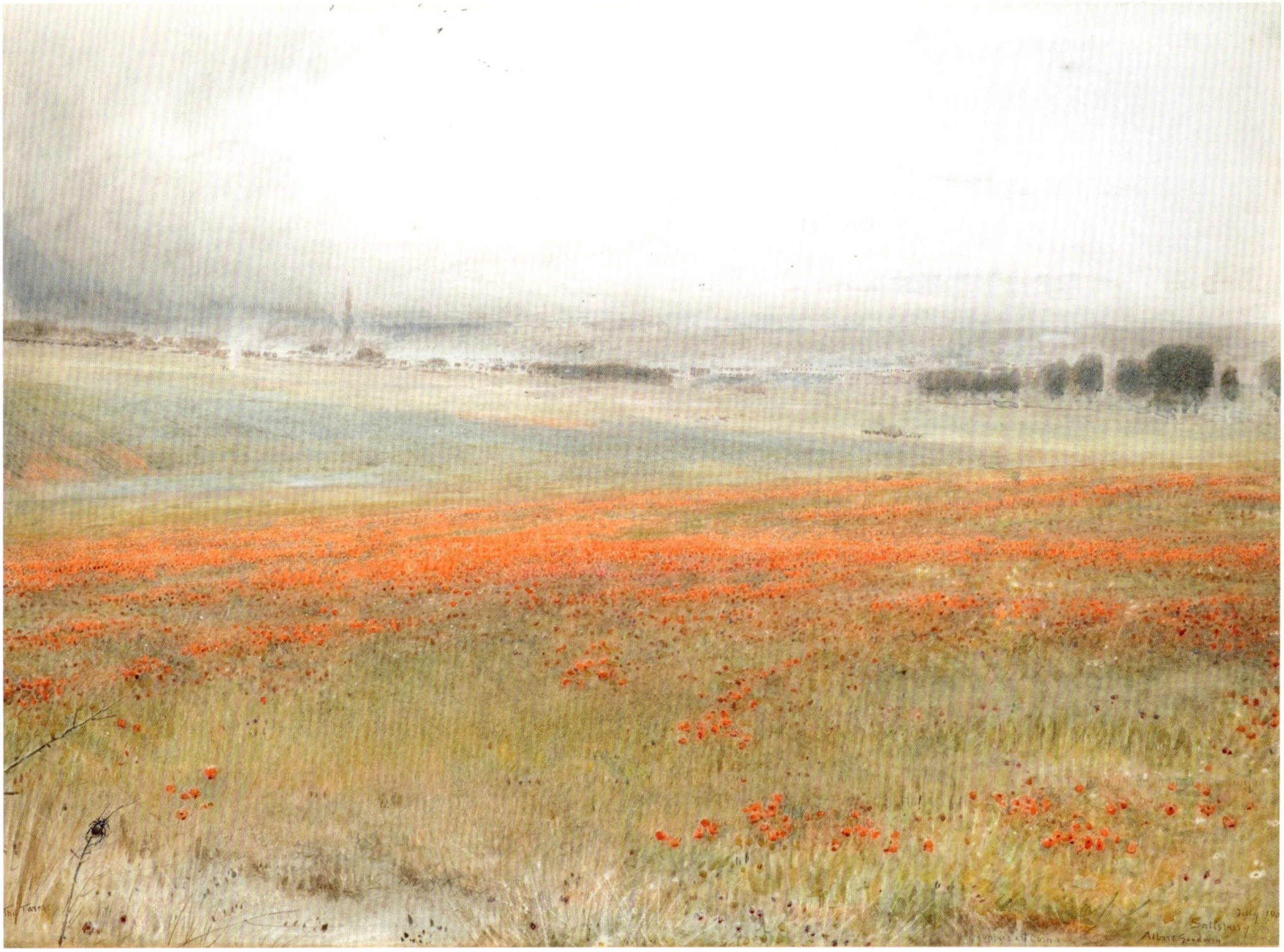

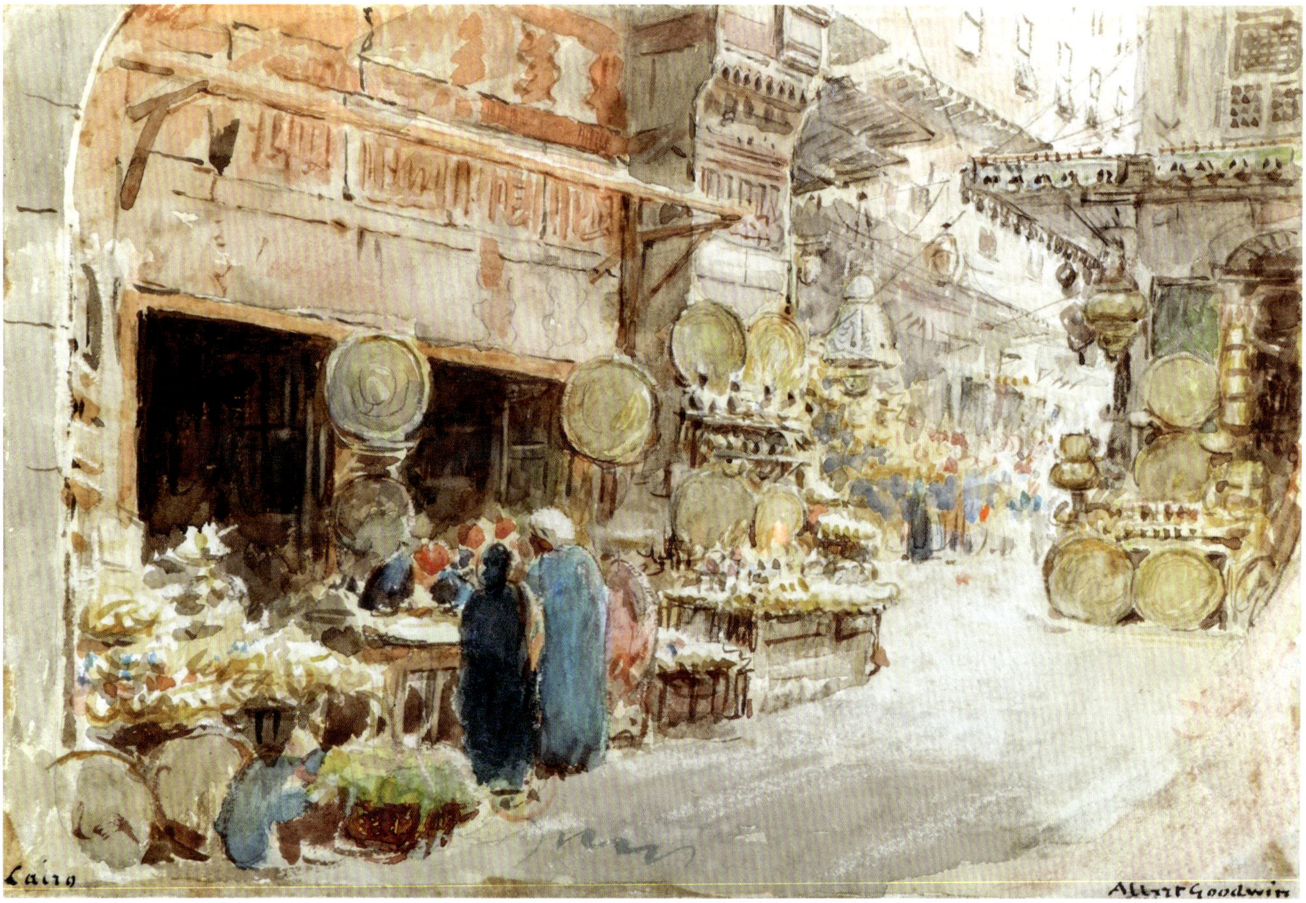

37 **Cairo**
Signed and inscribed with title
Watercolour with pencil
6 ¾ x 9 ¾ inches

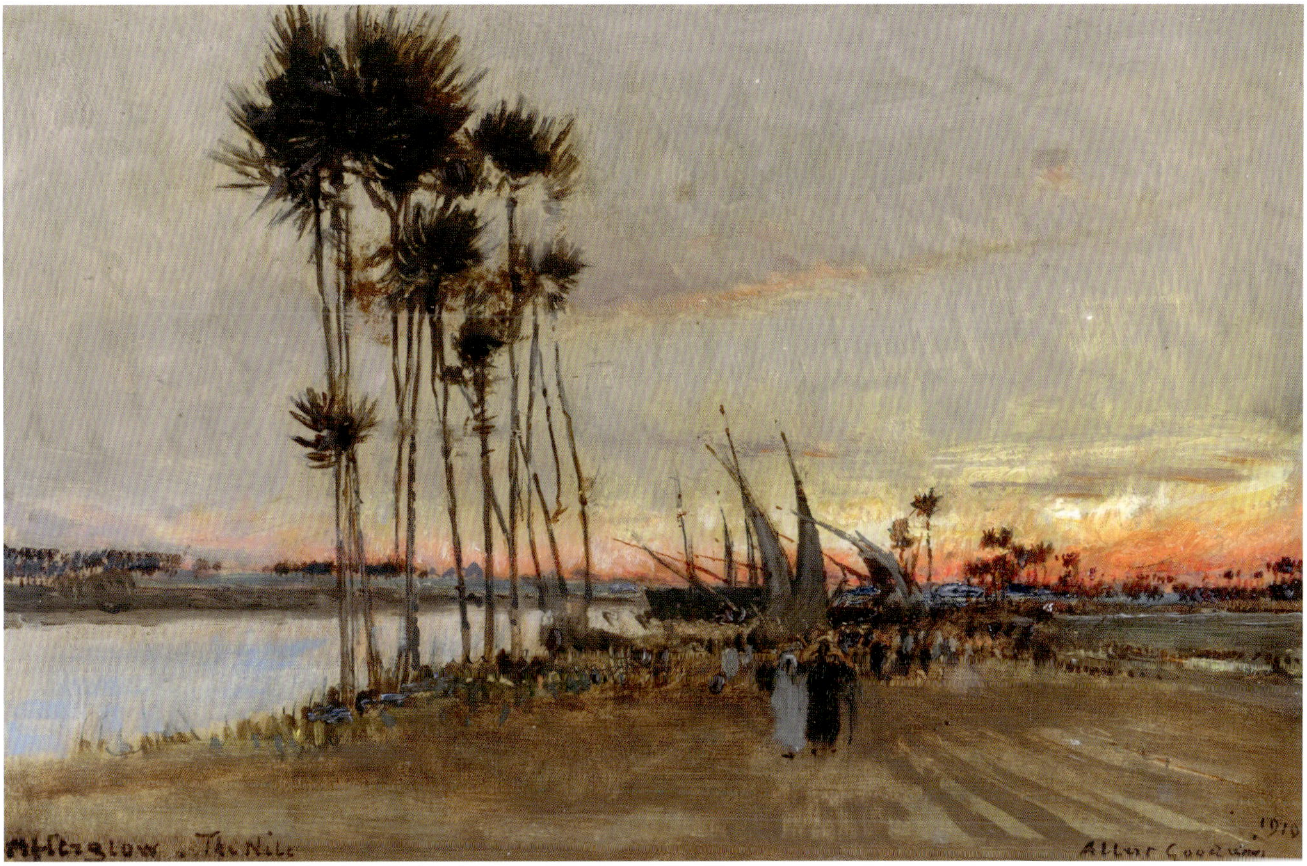

38 **Afterglow. The Nile**
Signed, inscribed with title and dated 1910
Oil on board
7 ½ x 11 inches

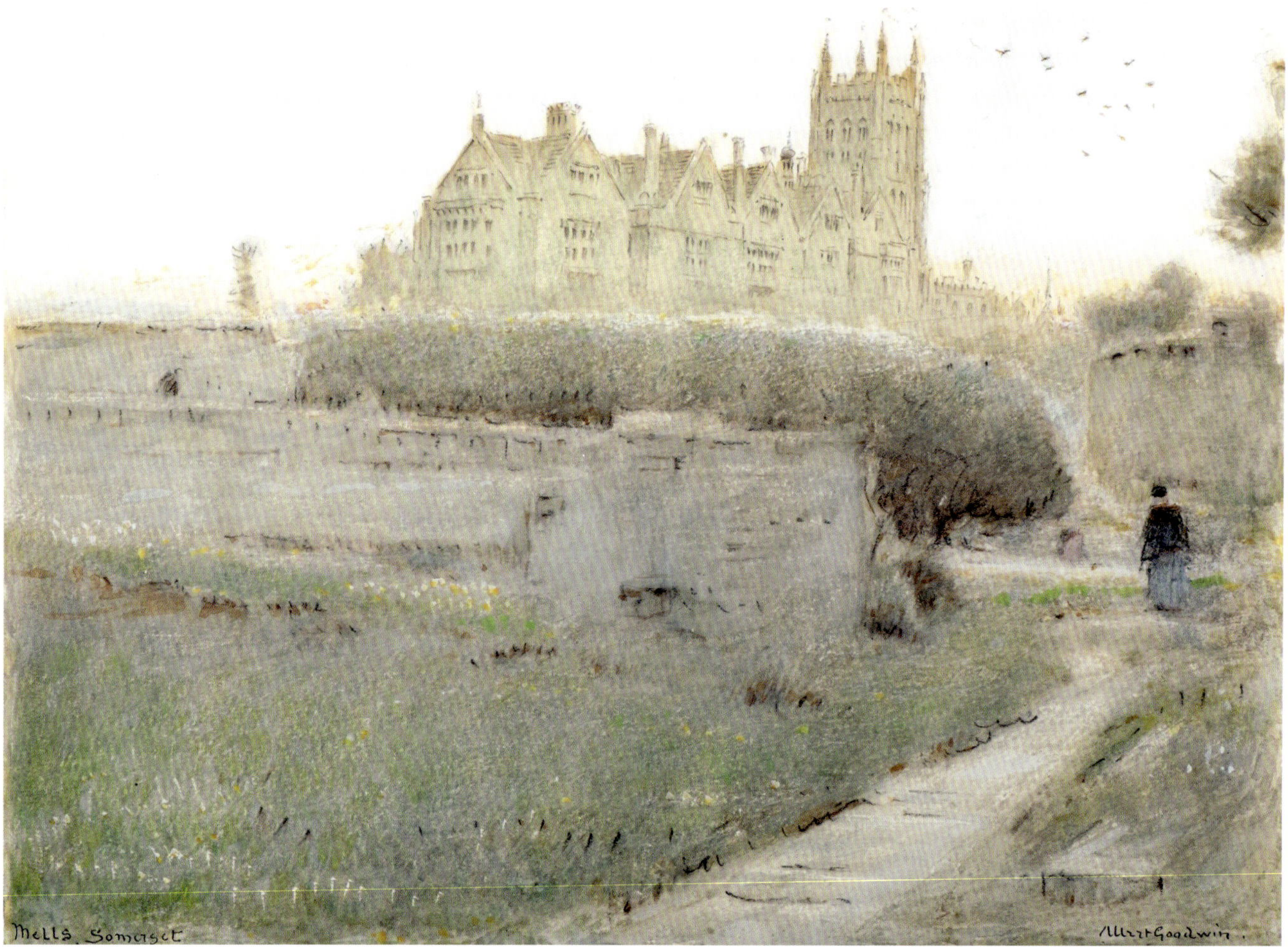

39 **Mells, Somerset**
Signed and inscribed with title
Watercolour with pencil
9 x 11 ¼ inches

St Andrew's church was predominantly built in the second half of the 15th century and later restored in the 19th century. In this painting St Andrew's tower, built in 1446, appears above and behind Mells Manor, built the 16th century for Edward Horner. Two thirds of the house was demolished around 1780 and the remaining third was restored by Sir Edwin Lutyens (a close friend of the Horners), around the time of this painting. Lutyens designed a Loggia with Tuscan columns and updated the interior to include new bathrooms and kitchens, as well heating and electrics. He also designed the gateposts in 1925 and several memorials within the church and village.

'Now I write from Winchester College, the guest of the Headmaster – M. Rendall – sort of cousin of my wife's. Came, partly to do some drawings for a presentation to a leaving Housemaster. Today has been one continual downpour – most depressing. Dined in Hall. Curious to think that not one boy who was part of the crowd of eaters with us today, was here when I was last doing the same thing – seven years ago! How quickly the generations pass!'

(*The Diary of Albert Goodwin, RWS, 1883-1927*, Privately Printed, 1934, Page 121, 28 October, 1909)

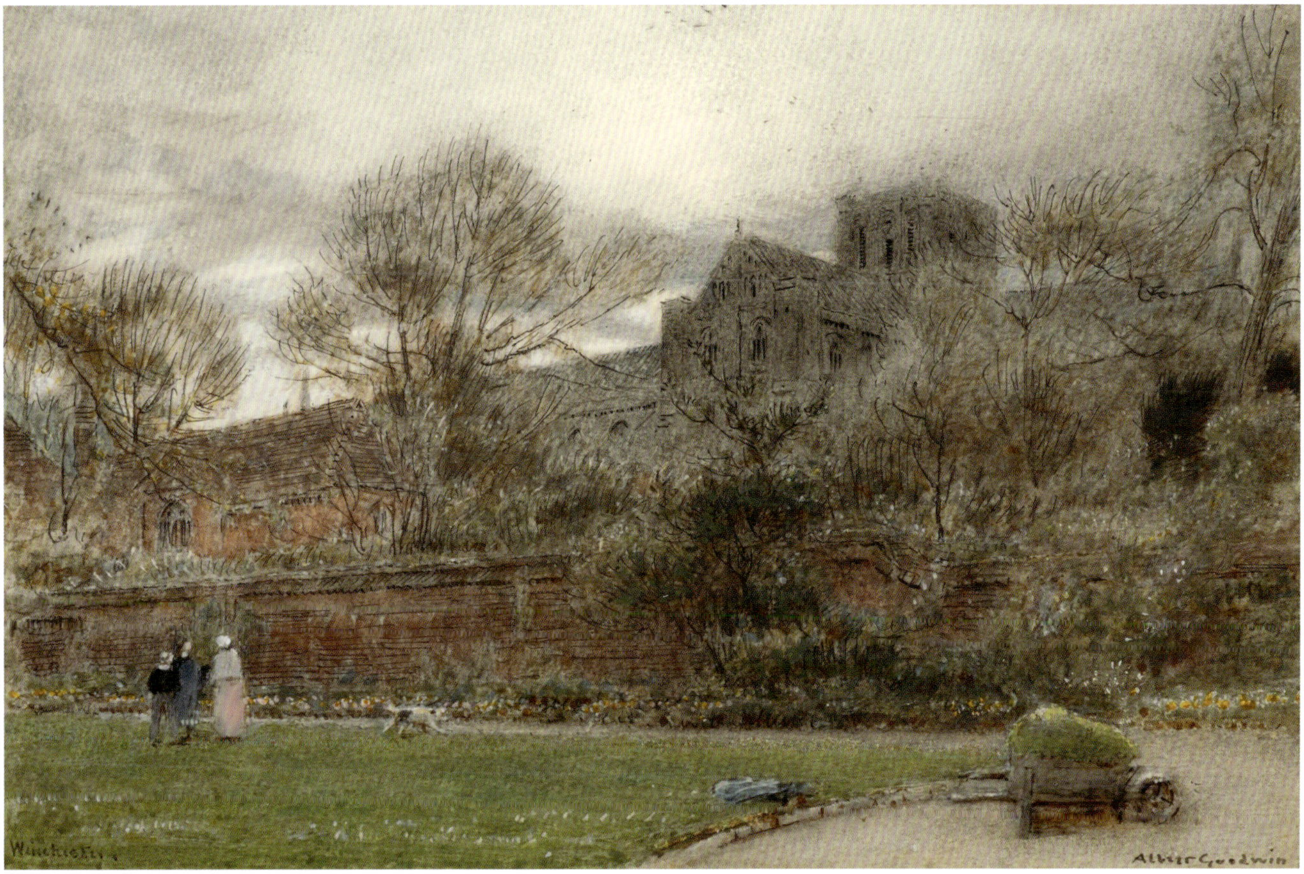

40 **Winchester**
Signed and inscribed with title
Watercolour with bodycolour
9 ¼ x 14 inches
Literature:
Hammond Smith, *Albert Goodwin RWS*, Leigh-on-Sea: F Lewis, 1977, Plate 7

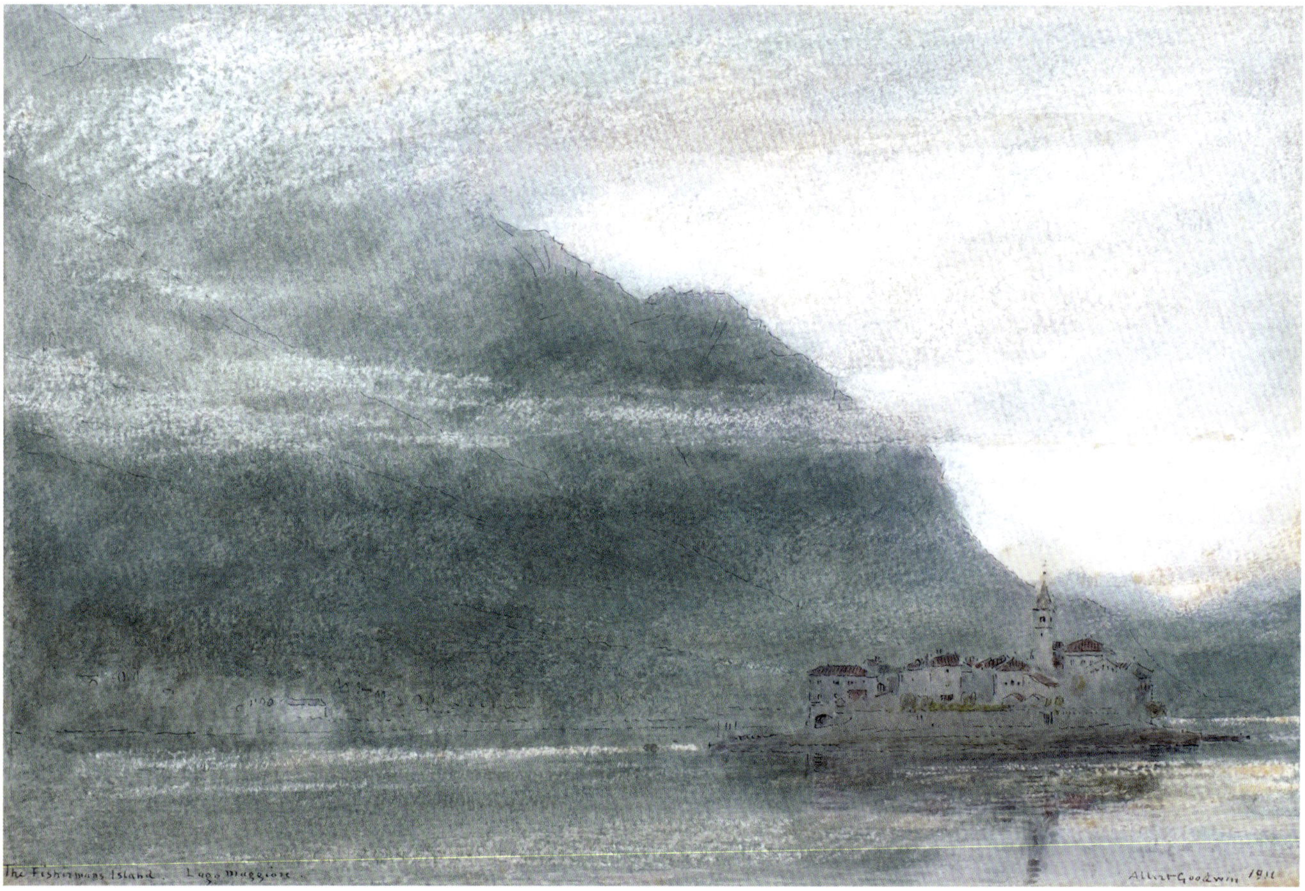

41 The Fishermans Island. Lago Maggiore
Signed, inscribed with title and dated 1911
Watercolour with pen and ink
7 ½ x 11 inches

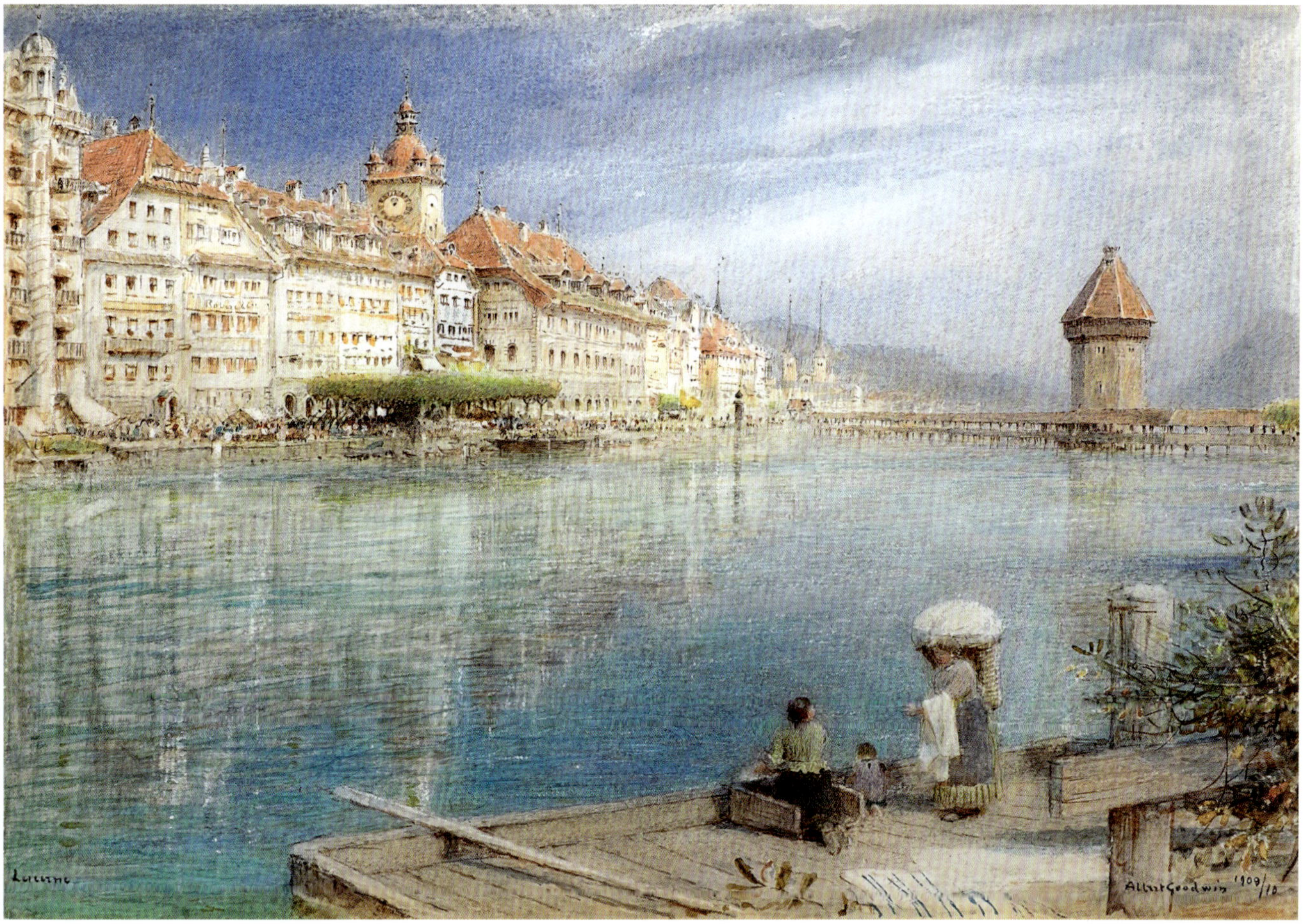

42 Lucerne

Signed, inscribed with title and dated 1909/10
Inscribed 'Frame at 30 St James St' on reverse
Signed and inscribed with title and 'no 3' on address label on backboard
Watercolour with pen and ink
10 ½ x 14 ¾ inches
Literature:
Albert Goodwin RWS, 1845-1932, London: Chris Beetles Ltd, 1986, Limited Edition of 1000, Plate 118
Exhibited:
A Museum Tour of the Royal Watercolour Society, Sheffield Mappin Art Gallery, Ruskin Gallery, Stoke on Trent City Museum and Art Gallery, May-October 1986, No 78;
'A Watercolourist's Dream. Albert Goodwin (1845-1932) & John Lewis Roget (1828-1908)', The County Gallery, Maidstone, February-March 1999

43 Westminster from Lambeth Bridge (below)
Signed, inscribed with title and dated 1912
Watercolour with pen and ink
13 ½ x 20 ½ inches
Literature:
Albert Goodwin RWS, 1845-1932, London: Chris Beetles Ltd, 1986, Limited Edition of 1000, Plate 140

44 Houses of Parliament (opposite)
Signed, inscribed 'Westminster' and dated 1912
Watercolour with bodycolour
21 x 26 inches
Literature:
Albert Goodwin RWS, 1845-1932, London: Chris Beetles Ltd, 1986, Limited Edition of 1000, Plate 141
Exhibited:
'Albert Goodwin RWS 1845-1932', Bolton Museum and Art Gallery, August-September 1981, and touring to Canterbury, Newcastle upon Tyne, Leicester and Sotheby's Belgravia, 1981-82, No 47;
'Albert Goodwin RWS 1845-1932. 129 of His Best Works Borrowed From Private Collections', a Museum Tour of the Royal Watercolour Society, Sheffield Mappin Art Gallery, Ruskin Gallery, Stoke on Trent City Museum and Art Gallery, May-October 1986, No 93

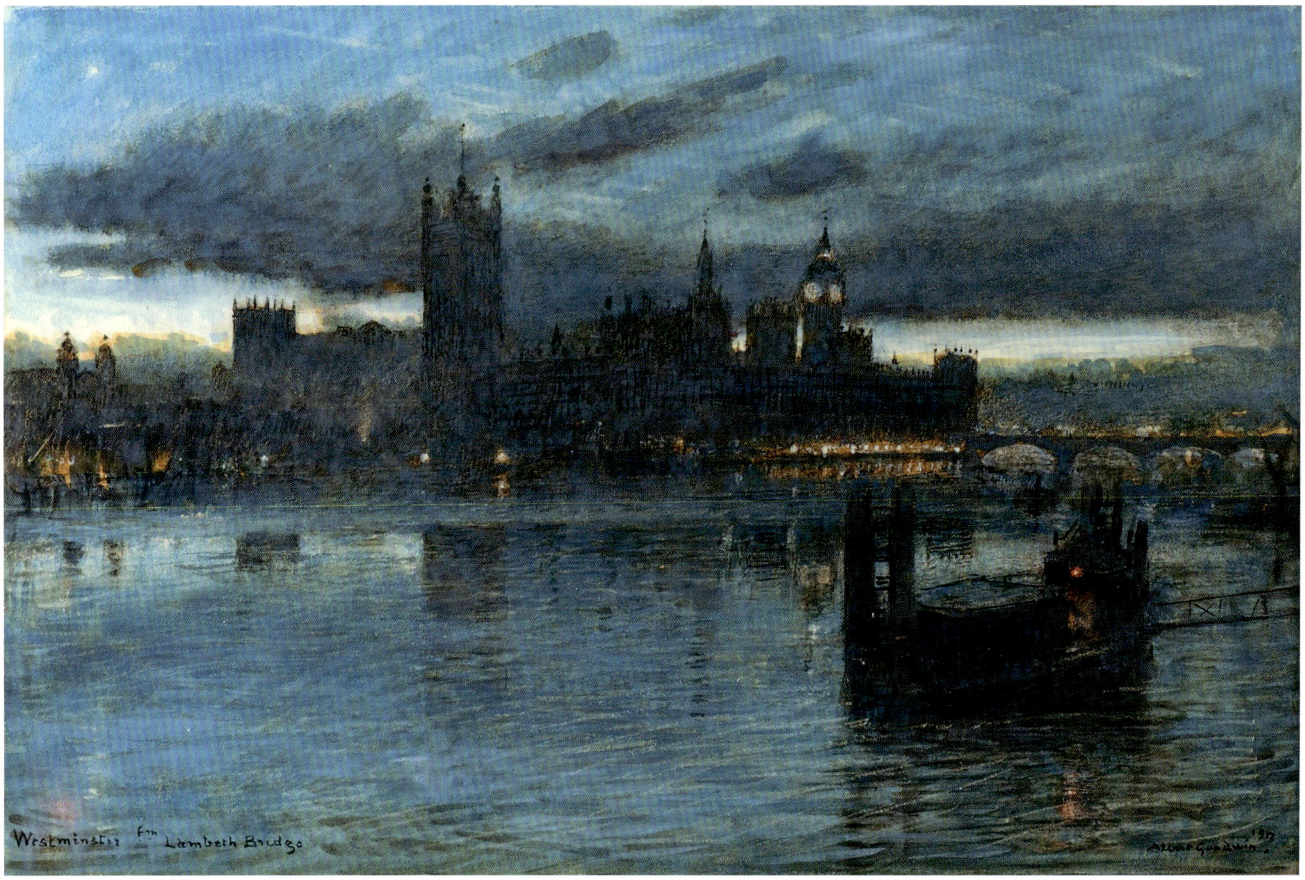

'Westminster and the River looked dirtily splendid, as I came through on my way back. A smoky sunset, behind the Houses of Parliament, giving the touch of colour the grimy city needed! The grime of London is an evil that emphasizes colour! It was that struck Whistler, the first to discover beauty in Wapping! Nature is far more economical with her colour scheme than we think. In the most gorgeous sunset, there is generally far less flinging about of crude paint than we imagine. Far more often, if we closely analyse the matter, is it seen that there is one vivid splash of pure primary colour, all else, repeating this, in lower and lower tones. But seldom is there more than one centre of pure, unadulterated colour, and with many such skies grey predominates throughout, framing each separate little bit of brightness. In fact Nature is always carrying about her frame-maker to show off, not only her larger pictures, but to separately frame and show off her scattered bits of the rainbow.'

(*The Diary of Albert Goodwin, RWS, 1883-1927*, Privately Printed, 1934, Page 300, 26 February 1915)

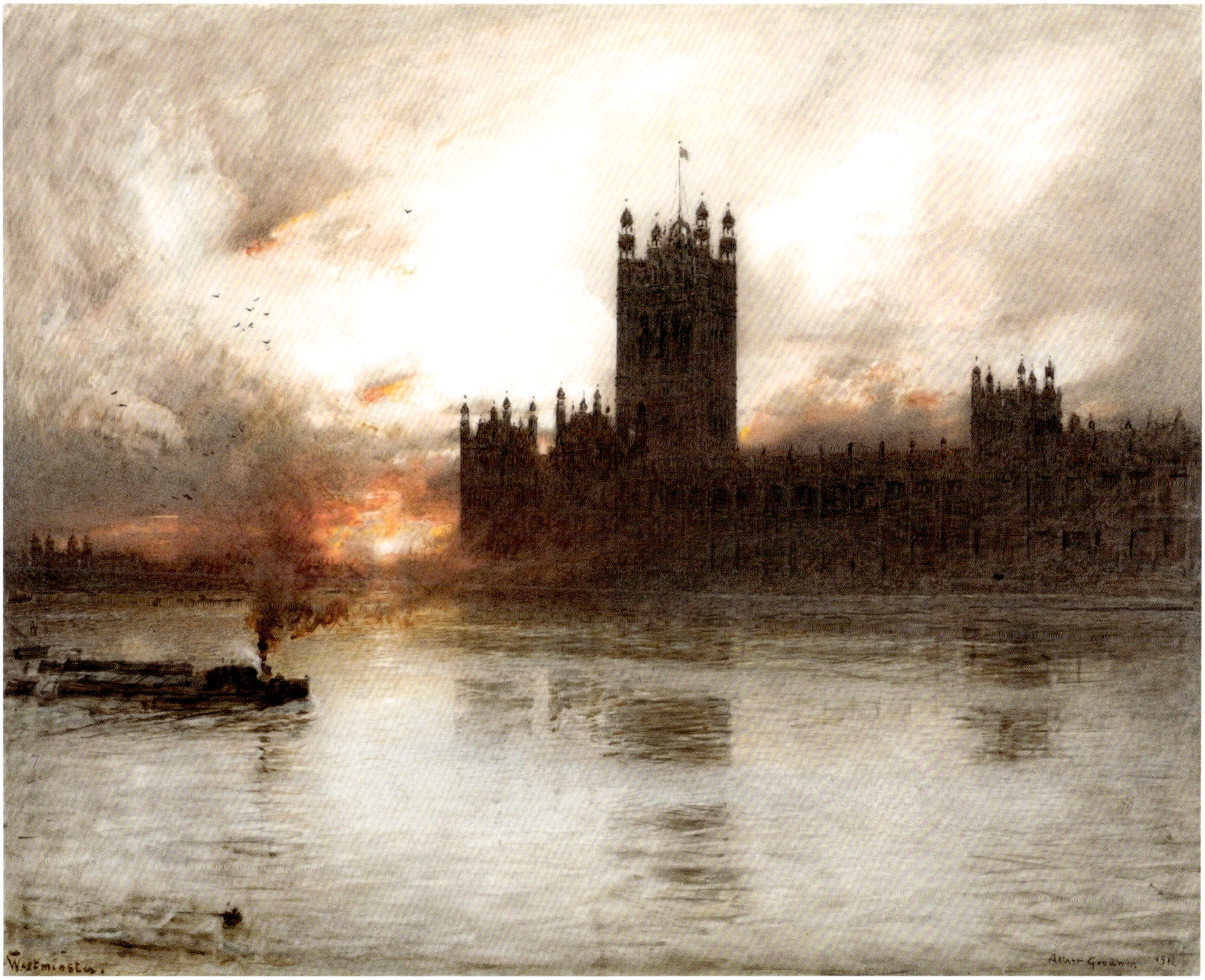

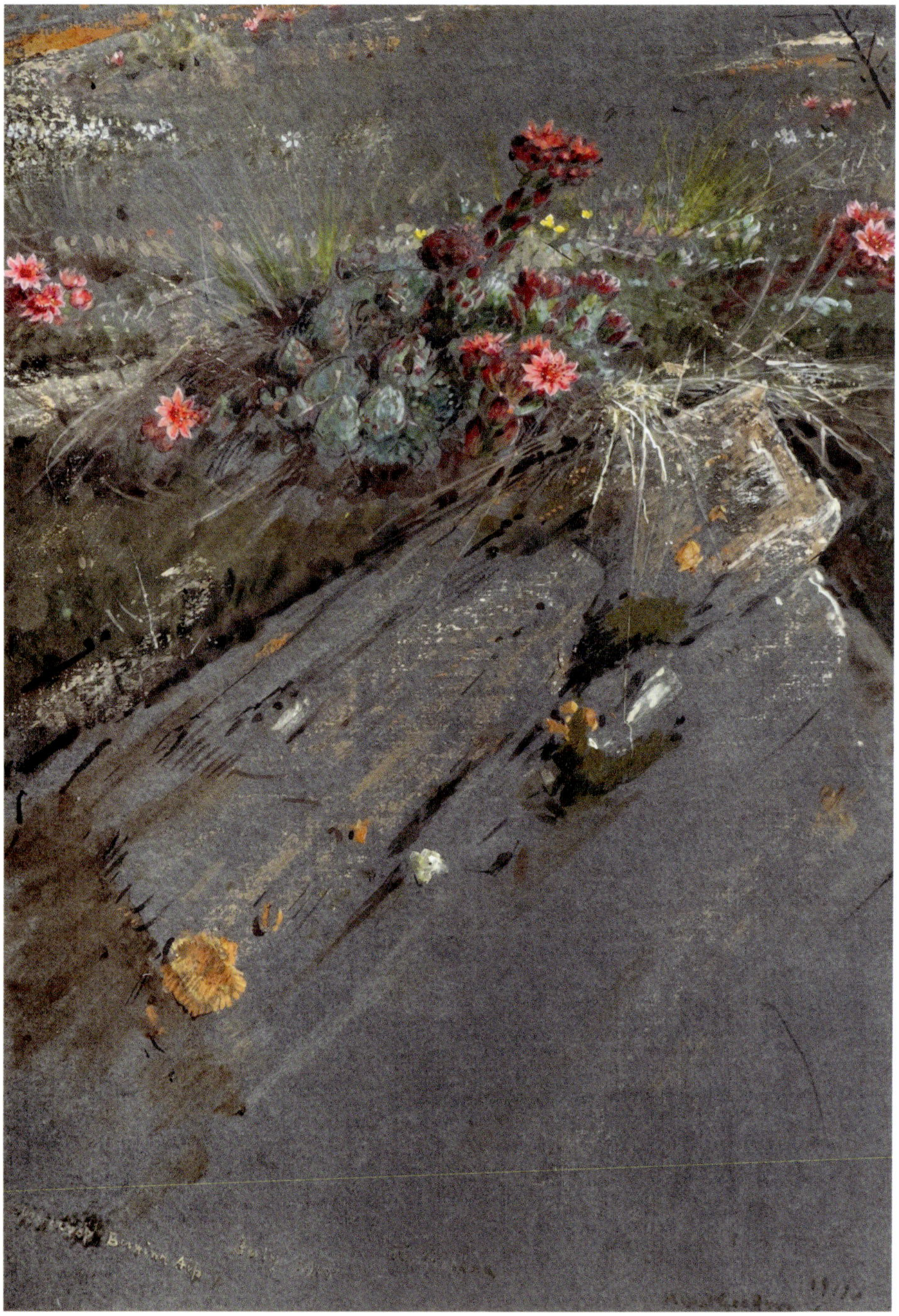

45 **Stonecrop, Bumina Alp, Pontresina July 1913**
Signed, inscribed with title and dated 1914
Watercolour and bodycolour on tinted paper
14 x 9 inches
Literature:
Albert Goodwin RWS, 1845-1932, London: Chris Beetles Ltd, 1986, Limited Edition of 1000, Plate 150
Exhibited:
'Albert Goodwin RWS 1845-1932. 129 of His Best Works Borrowed From Private Collections',
a Museum Tour of the Royal Watercolour Society, Sheffield Mappin Art Gallery, Ruskin Gallery,
Stoke on Trent City Museum and Art Gallery, May-October 1986, No 100

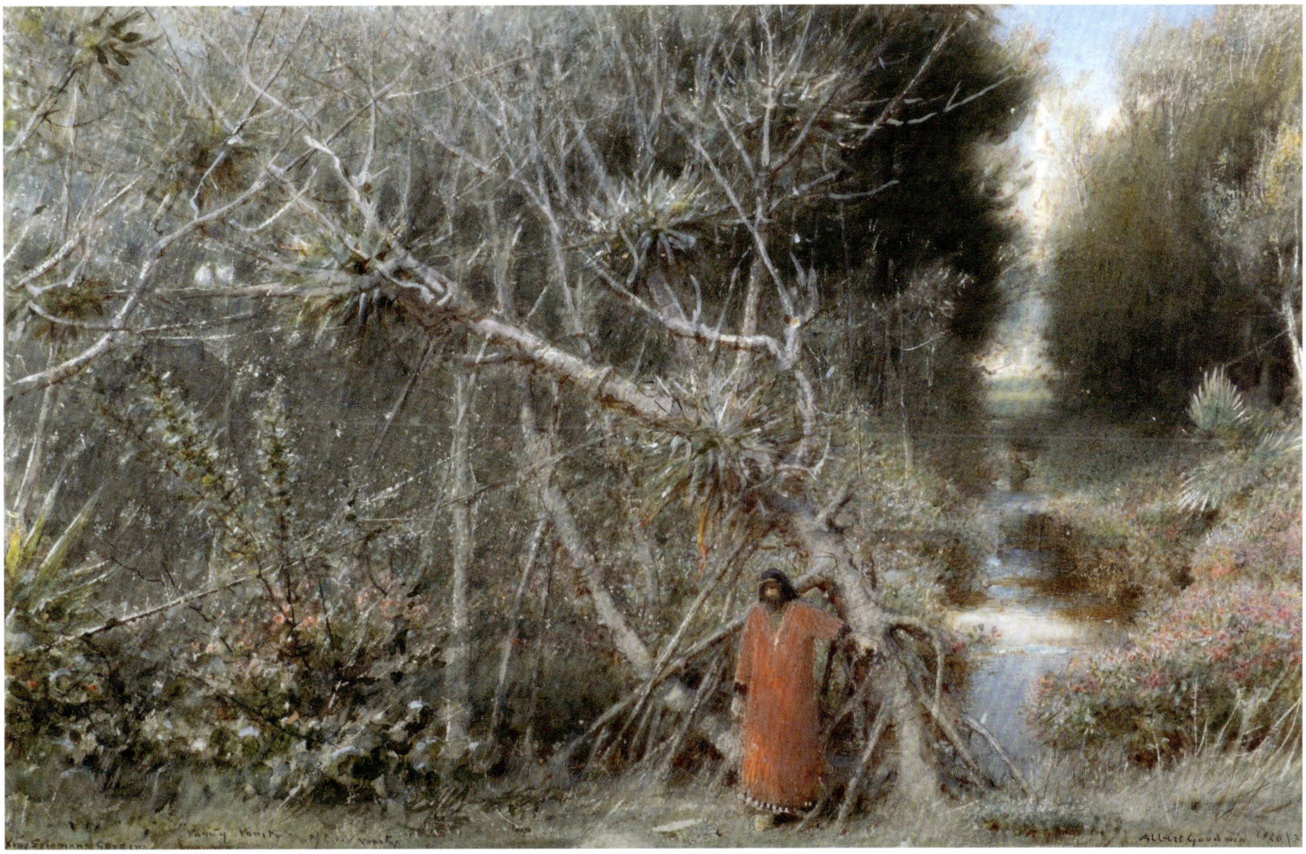

46 King Solomon's Garden. 'Vanity Vanity All Is Vanity'

Signed, inscribed with title and dated 1920/21

Watercolour and bodycolour

13 x 19 ½ inches

Literature:

Albert Goodwin RWS, 1845-1932, London: Chris Beetles Ltd, 1986, Limited Edition of 1000, Plate 192

Exhibited:

Royal Society of Painters in Water-colours, 1921, no 43;

'Albert Goodwin RWS 1845-1932. 129 of His Best Works Borrowed From Private Collections.
A Museum Tour of the Royal Watercolour Society, Sheffield Mappin Art Gallery, Ruskin Gallery, Stoke on Trent City Museum and Art Gallery, May-October 1986, No 124;

'A Watercolourist's Dream', The County Gallery, Maidstone, February 1999

'Began this evening drawing of Benares, a commission for a replica of one in b drawings sold to Sir T. L. Devitt — or rather exchanged for my return ticket to New Zealand — a friend of his seeing the book and in it the drawing got his permission to allow make a larger one of the same subject. Commissions are so rare nowadays that I am ashamed I have put off the doing of this TO DO long, but now that November weather has come with the 5th, I have no excuse for any further attempts at out-o'-doors painting, which is now impossible. My work in that way must be done from the vantage-ground of friendly windows, and what a wealth of work can be done from that: how many I got out of my cabin window on the sea. At sea and in port, last year at this time.

I saw Benares for two days — I think each day from the river where I had engaged a sort of house-boat with a guide who was anxious to show his credentials, and for me to add my testimony to the many names in his book of them, among others that of Val Prinsep, the painter. The Val that Rossetti's rhyme made at the time when the Frescoes at the "Union" in Oxford were being painted, comes into my mind, and was rather full of Rossetti s good-natured admiring contempt for the enormous man with a child's name:

"There was a young fellow named Val,
The roughs' and the prize-fighters' pal;
The head of a broom and the brains of a groom
Were the gifts Heaven granted to Val."

This guide was a learned pundit and was a very superior person with a contemptuous tolerance for the Christian religion which I gathered he considered a little inferior to Buddhism! but he allowed it was on the same lines!

He was an expensive luxury but I had to disregard expense, for I needed him to arrange the hire of the boat, the two men to manage it when I wanted to stop and draw, and all other details; he was useful, too, in telling me things which I otherwise should have been puzzled over. One thing I saw under the enormously tall minarets of the only Mohammedan mosque in Benares, and that was half-way between the Ganges and it – a huge, great coal-black pillar, just like an old pine-cone stuck (blunt end downwards) on to a stone pillar — the whole thing, I suppose, forty feet high. This I could not make out the meaning of, nor why it should be in contrast to the brownish yellow stone of most of the buildings. He explained it was for the time of festivals when at night the place was illuminated. Thus I understood I was too far off to see the detail, but gathered it and saw in my mind the effect, for this was a huge candle, or would look line one, when at night would be fitted with thousands of oil lamps, and the whole when lighted would make a thirty-feet flame. It struck me at once how this would look in the moonlight, with this domination of the commanding mosque, whose gigantic minarets would stand out bluey white against an indigo sky behind it, while down below in the murk and smoke while of all the lesser lights this great torch would light up the whole scene.

Afterwards I — from the outline made in the house-boat — painted this imaginary moonlight in the time of the festival which I could not see for I had only a short two days to get notes. All the time I was, I felt, getting ready for the fever which I was sure had been steadily pursuing me during my last week or two in India. I know the two days' work and the two days' crushing weight of all the astonishment and wonder of the sight of kaleidoscopic Benares (bathing in full action) so took the life out of me that I felt I could not stand another day and took an enormous dose of quinine and went to bed, and with that "lift up" the next day I started home.'

(*The Diary of Albert Goodwin, RWS, 1883-1927*, Privately Printed, 1934, Pages 362 & 363, 5 November 1917)

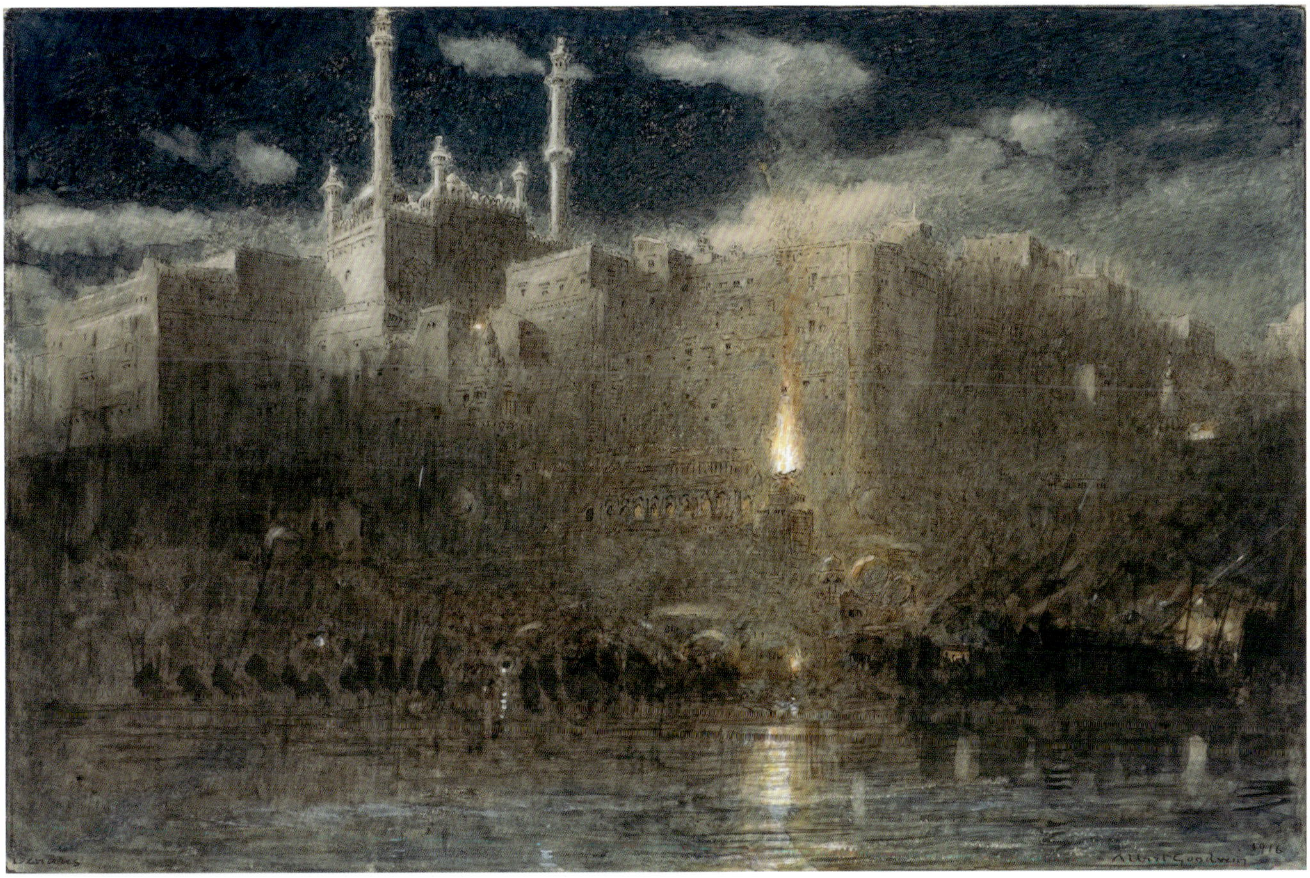

47 Benares by Moonlight

Signed, inscribed 'Benares' and dated 1916

Watercolour and bodycolour with pen and ink

9 ½ x 14 inches

Exhibited: 'Chris Beetles Summer Show', Chris Beetles Gallery, London, 2006, No 28

'... note the startling visual angles from which Goodwin often works. This is not a man content, as were the mass of Victorian topographers, with the banality of the level horizon, with inchoate groping at the picturesque and sublime by snapshots up to misty mountain-tops. Beachy Head *is painted from a steep and plunging Japanese point of vision. Often, too, his compositions shift the main focus of the painting one plane to the side.'*

(Godfrey Barker, 'Why Albert Goodwin Matters', *Albert Goodwin RWS 1845-1932*, London: Chris Beetles Ltd, 2007, Page 8)

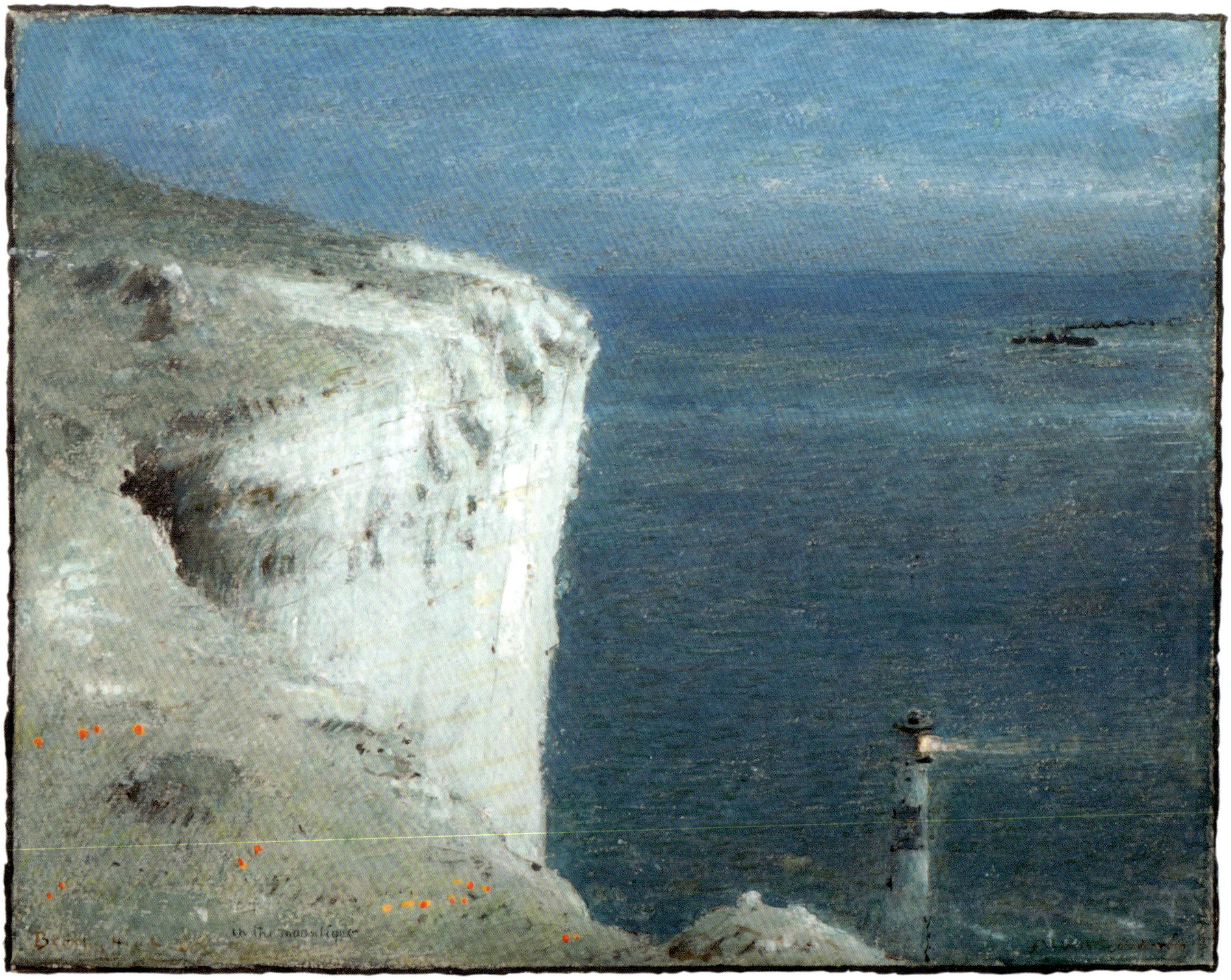

48 **Beachy Head in the Moonlight**
Signed and inscribed with title
Watercolour and bodycolour
9 ½ x 12 inches

'Half the day spent in painting, the other half in a delightful motor drive to Bideford: they dropped me at Instow, where in perfect conditions of temperature and weather I had an hour and a half's drawing of old Appledore. The skies to-day were more perfect than ever, from dawn to twilight, one continued banquet! What feasting I have had all my life in this way!'

(*The Diary of Albert Goodwin, RWS, 1883-1927*, Privately Printed, 1934, Page 337, 11 October 1915)

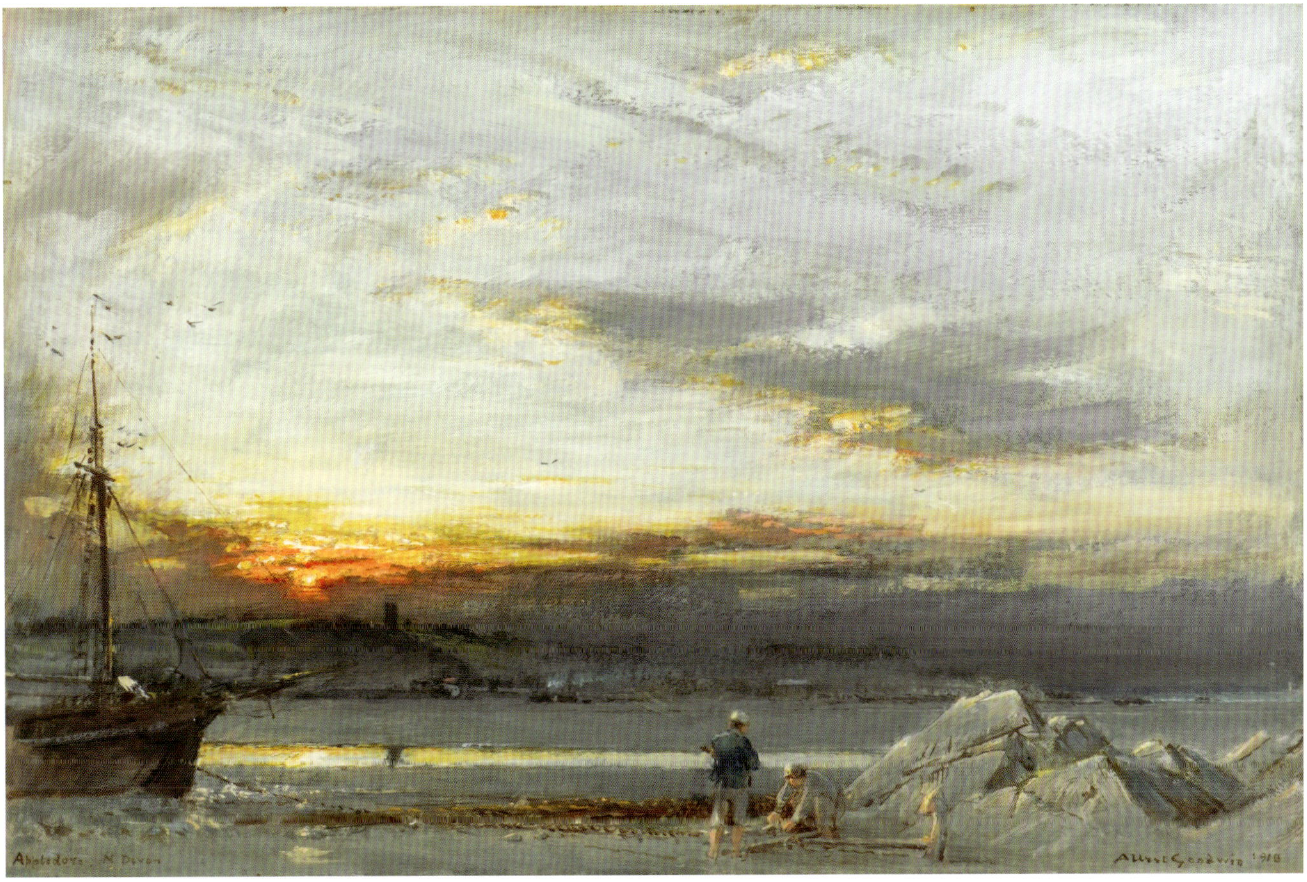

49 **Appledore, N Devon**
Signed, inscribed with title and dated 1918
Oil, watercolour and bodycolour on paper
13 ¾ x 20 ½ inches
Literature:
Albert Goodwin RWS, 1845-1932, London: Chris Beetles Ltd, 1986, Limited Edition of 1000, Plate 181
Exhibited:
'Drawings and Pictures by Albert Goodwin, RWS', Leggatt Brothers' Gallery, London, 1908, no 51;
'Albert Goodwin RWS 1845-1932. 129 of His Best Works Borrowed From Private Collections. A Museum Tour of the Royal Watercolour Society', Sheffield Mappin Art Gallery, Ruskin Gallery, Stoke on Trent City Museum and Art Gallery, May-October 1986, No 118

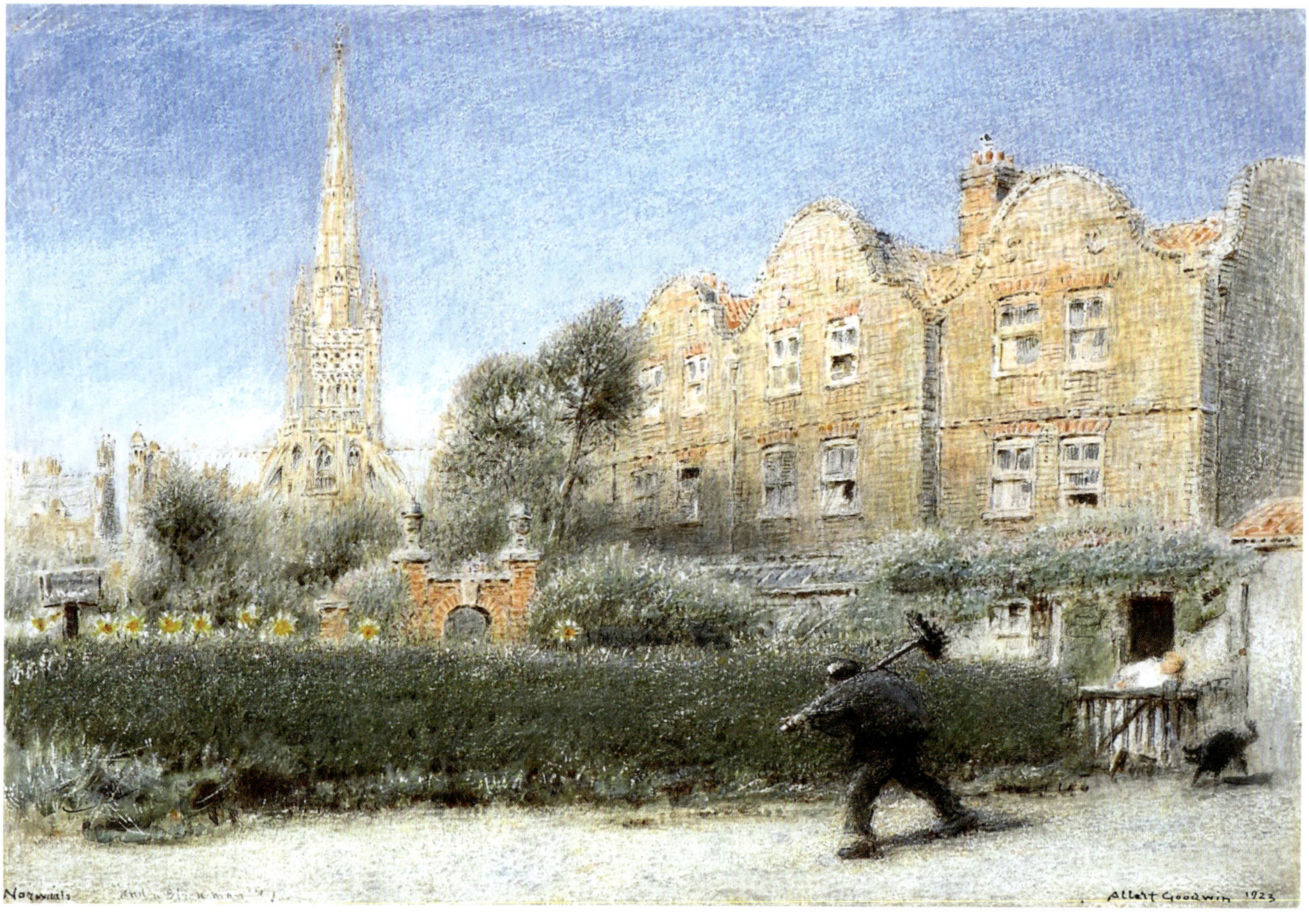

50 **Norwich "And a Black man"!**
Signed, inscribed with title and dated 1923
Watercolour with bodycolour
10 ½ x 15 inches
Literature:
Albert Goodwin RWS, 1845-1932, London: Chris Beetles Ltd, 1986,
Limited Edition of 1000, Plate 116 (similar, but with the sweep omitted)

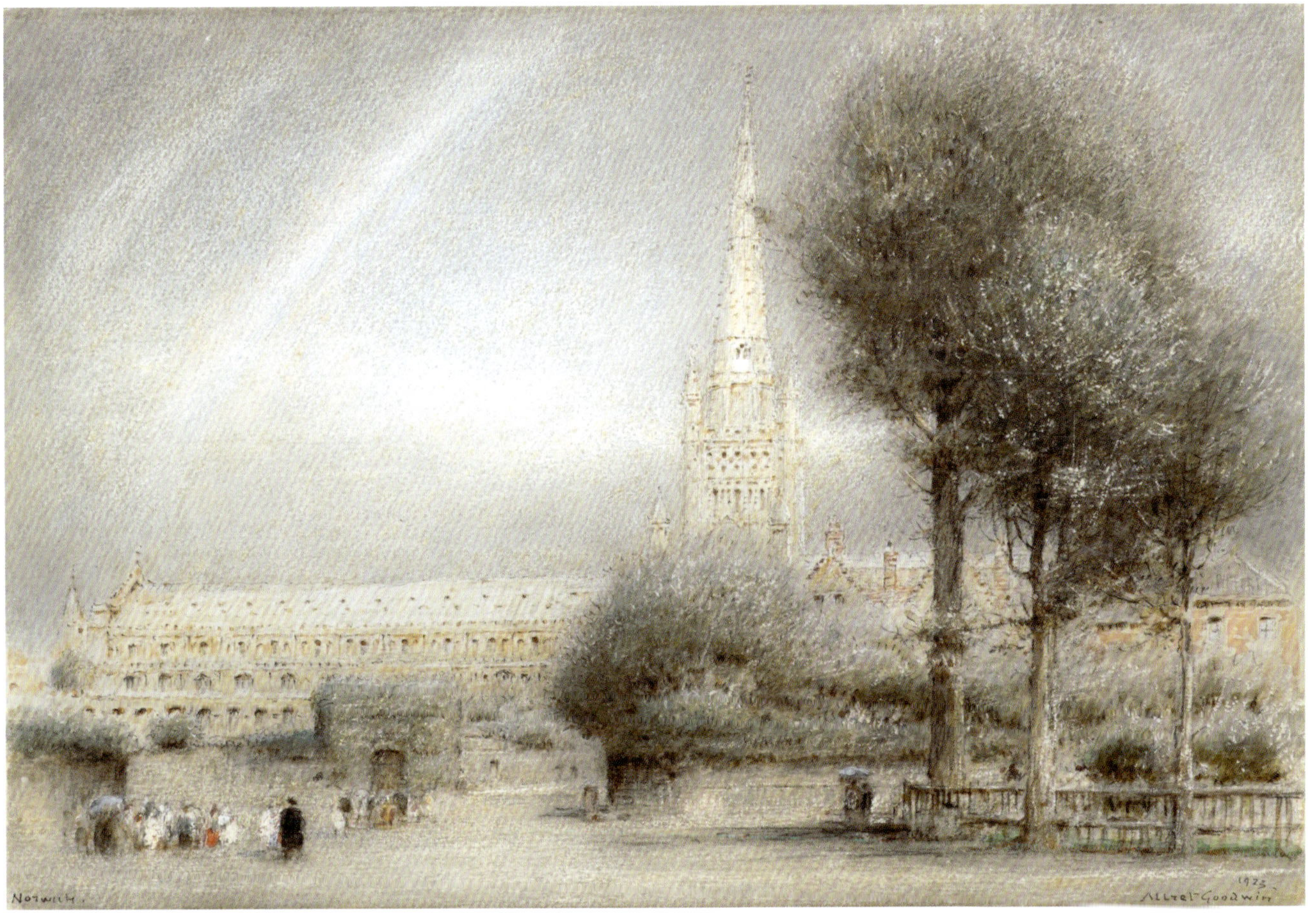

51 **Norwich Cathedral in Winter**
Signed, inscribed with title and dated 1923
Watercolour
10 ½ x 15 inches
Literature:
Albert Goodwin RWS, 1845-1932, London: Chris Beetles Ltd, 1986,
Limited Edition of 1000, Plate 199
Exhibited:
'Albert Goodwin RWS 1845-1932. 129 of His Best Works Borrowed From Private Collections.
A Museum Tour of the Royal Watercolour Society', Sheffield Mappin Art Gallery, Ruskin Gallery,
Stoke on Trent City Museum and Art Gallery, May-October 1986, No 128

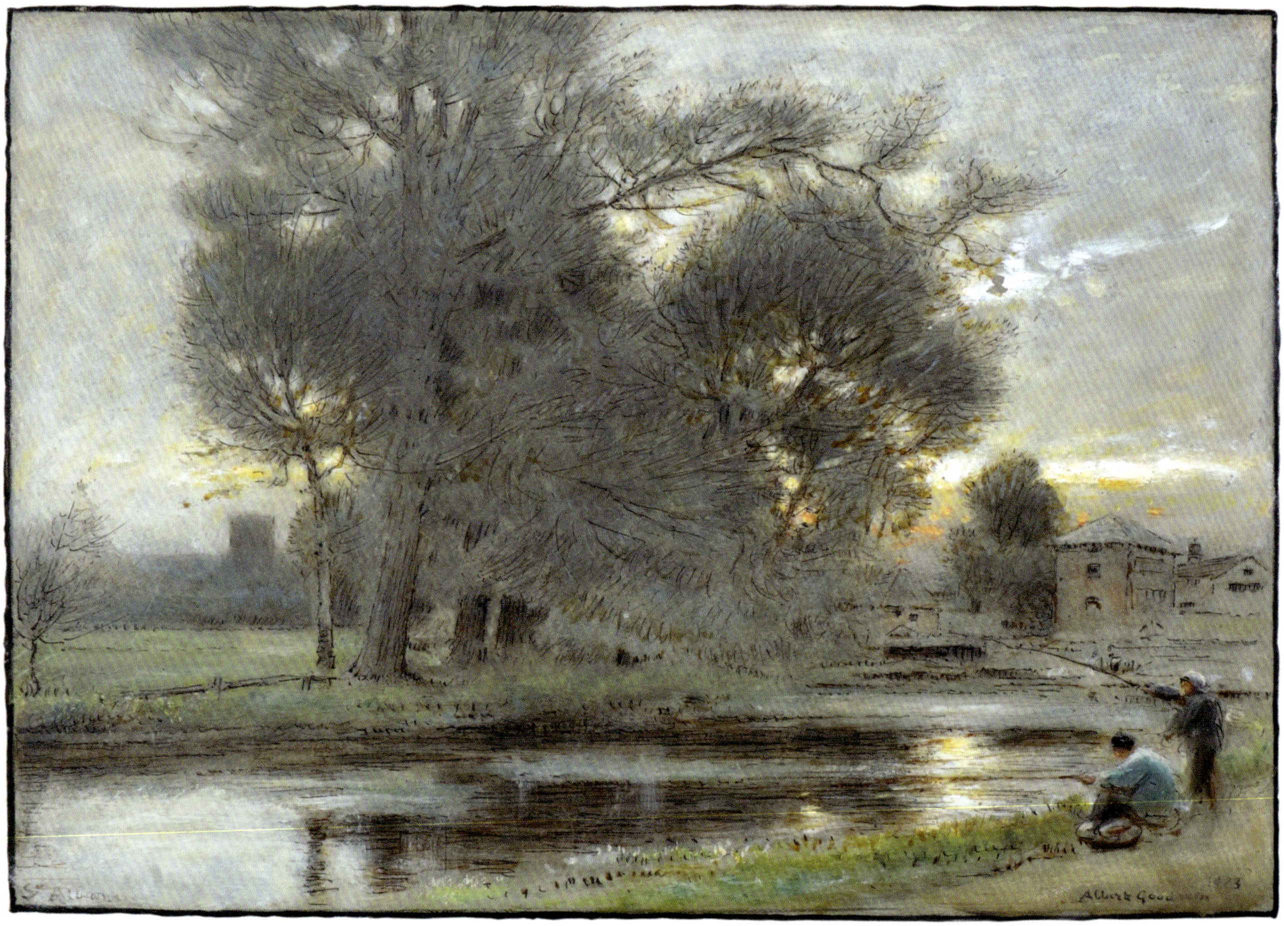

52 **St Albans**
Signed, inscribed with title and dated 1923
Watercolour, bodycolour and ink on tinted paper
11 ½ x 15 ½ inches

'Goodwin possessed an extraordinary gift for modelling landscape with the sponge in single colours and lower and lower tones, using pen to delineate form during and at the end of the process, never at the start. After Turner, no other watercolourist laid down giant zones of abstract colour with such sureness. It looks to be effortless; but when Lord Clark – Sir Kenneth Clark – went sketching with him in 1913 and 1914 and sought to imitate his methods, which Clark usefully describes, he achieved only "mechanical" results.'

(Godfrey Barker, 'Why Albert Goodwin Matters', *Albert Goodwin RWS 1845-1932*, London: Chris Beetles Ltd, 2007, Page 8)

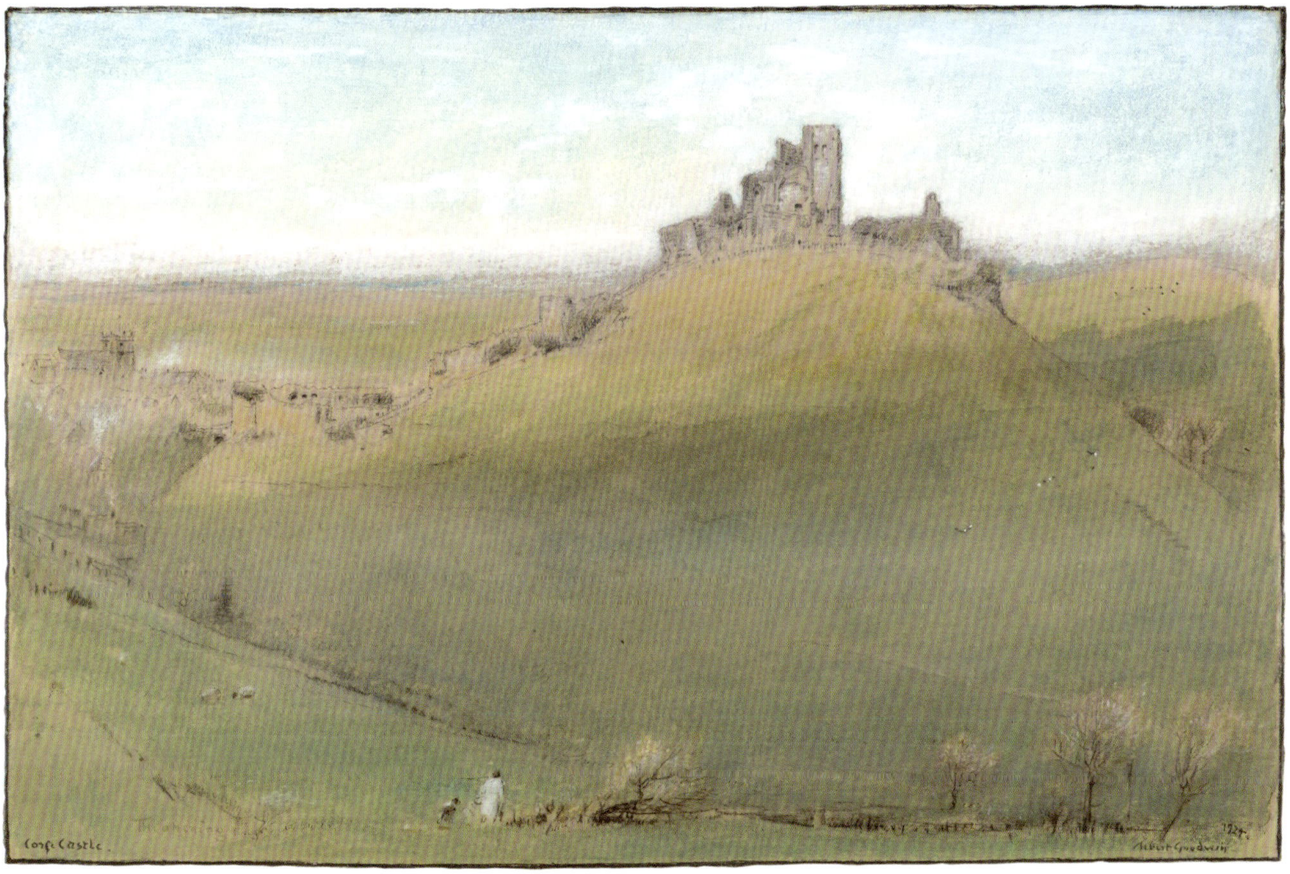

53 **Corfe Castle, The Opening Day**
Signed, inscribed with title and dated 1924
Watercolour with bodycolour, black chalk and ink on tinted paper
15 x 22 ½ inches
Literature:
Hammond Smith, *Albert Goodwin RWS*, Leigh-on-Sea: F Lewis, 1977, Plate 39

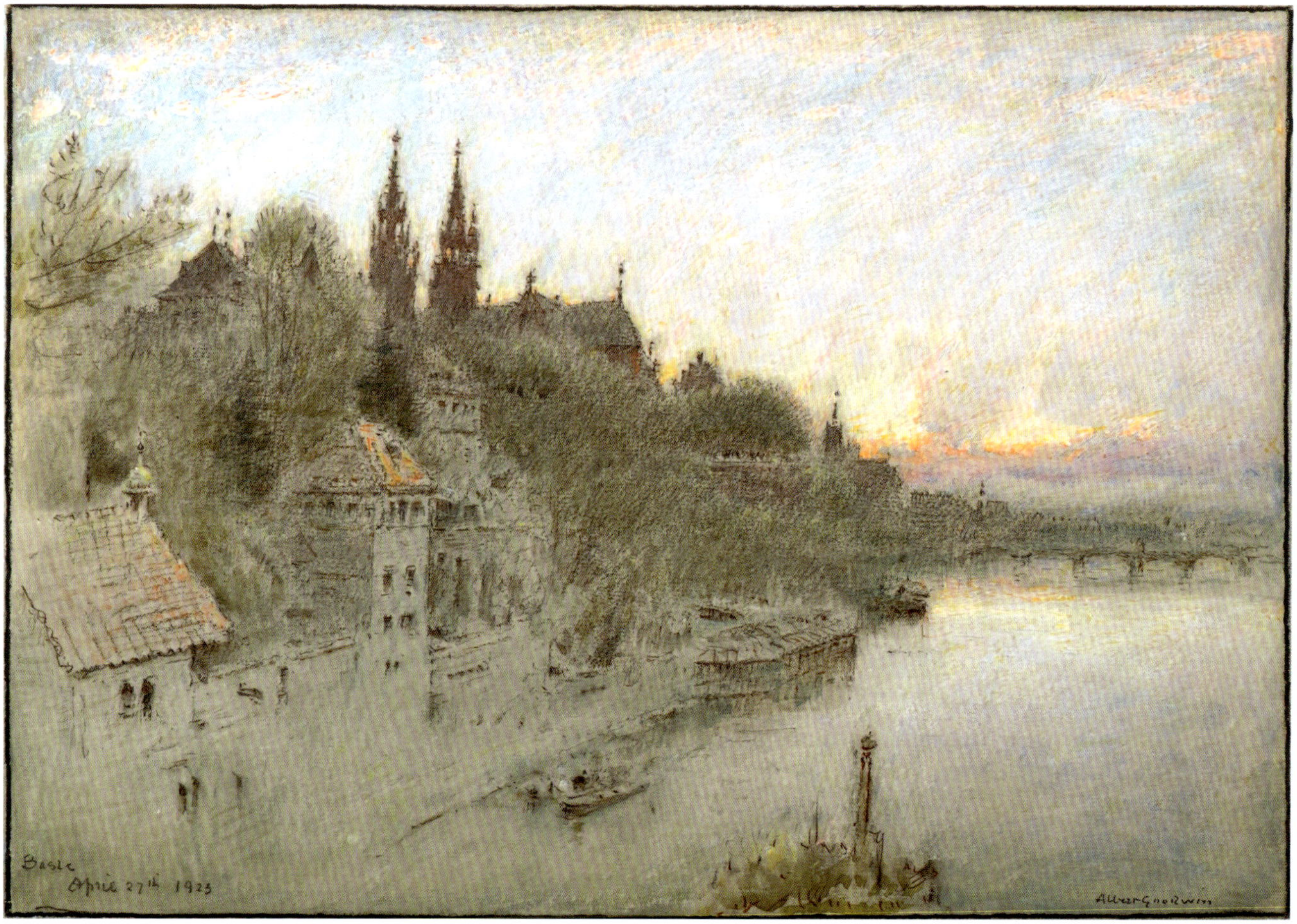

54 **Basle**
Signed, inscribed with title and dated 'April 27th 1923'
Watercolour with ink on tinted paper
10 ¼ x 14 inches

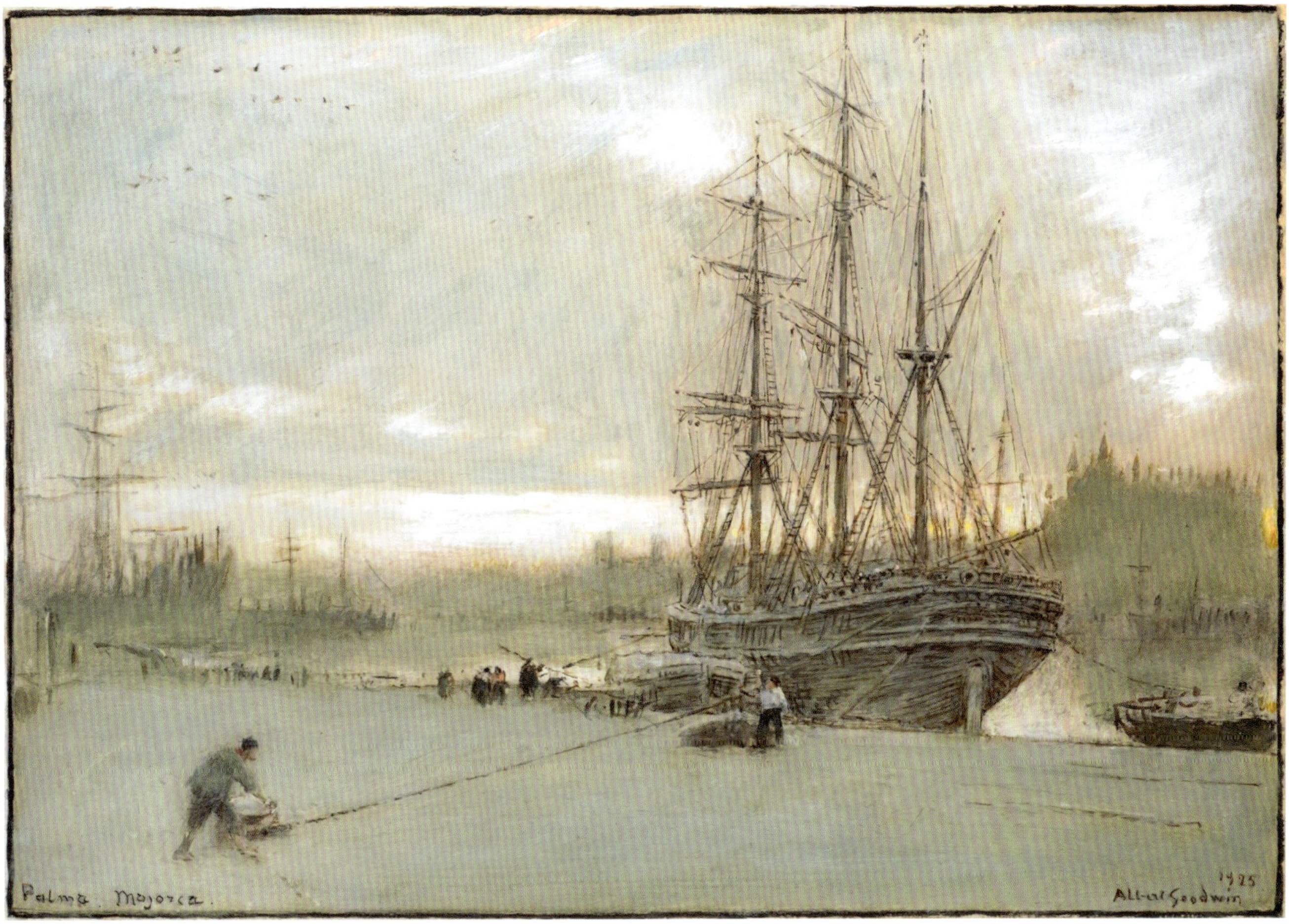

55 **Palma, Majorca**
Signed, inscribed with title and dated 1925
Oil, watercolour, bodycolour and ink
10 ¾ x 14 ¾ inches

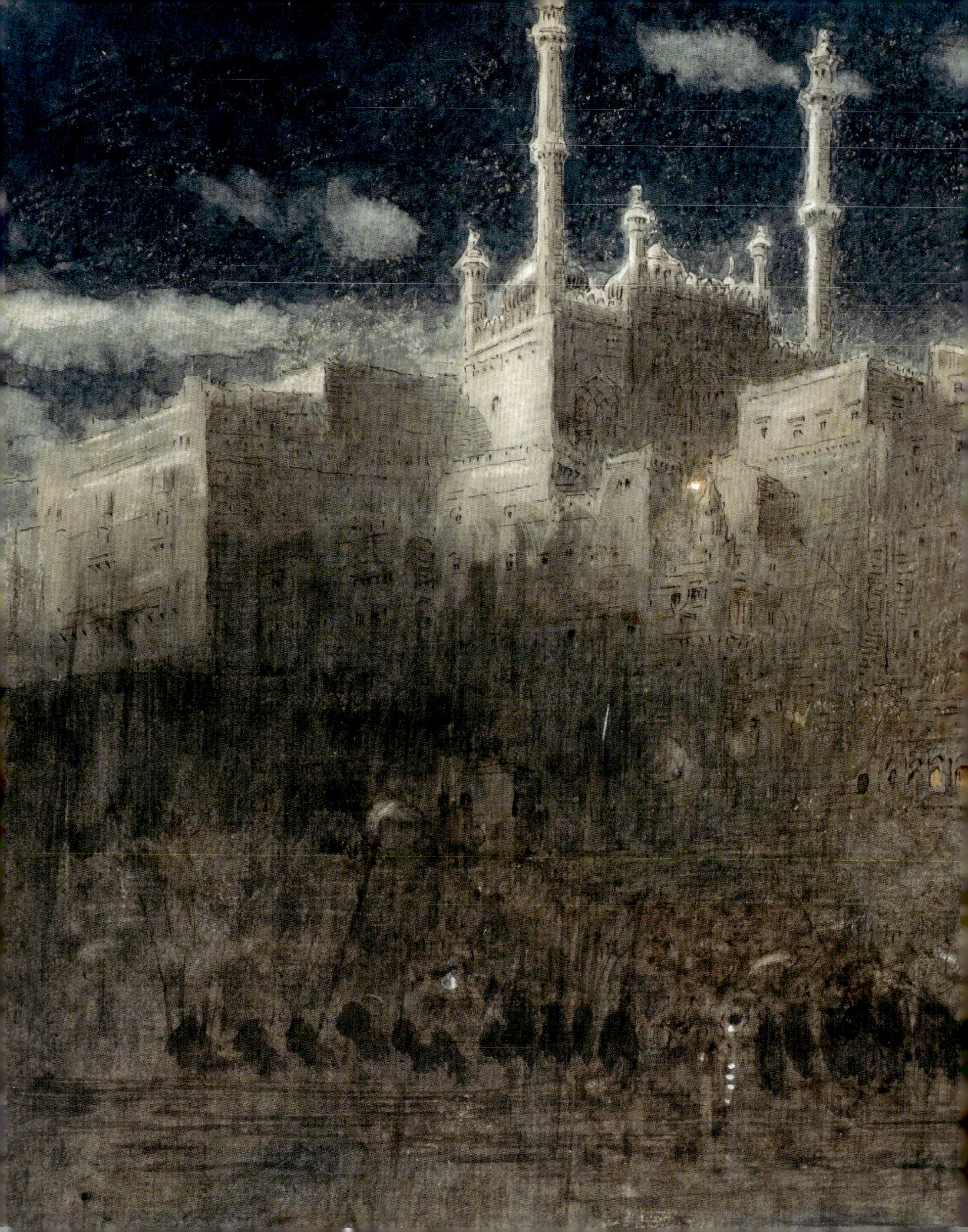